Formerly titled *Through the Valley of the Kwai* and *Miracle at the River Kwai*

A TRUE STORY
ABOUT THE WILL TO SURVIVE
AND THE COURAGE TO FORGIVE

TO END ALL WARS

ERNEST GORDON

GRAND RAPIDS, MICHIGAN 49530 USA

We want to hear from you. Please send your comments about this
book to us in care of the address below. Thank you.

GRAND RAPIDS, MICHIGAN 49530 USA

WWW.ZONDERVAN.COM

At the request of my children,
Gillian Margaret and Alastair James,
this book is dedicated to those who were my comrades
in the prison camps of the Railroad of Death

ZONDERVAN™

To End All Wars
Copyright © 1963 Ernest Gordon

First published in Great Britain in 1963 by Wm Collins Sons & Co. under the title
Through the Valley of the Kwai and in 1965 by Fontana/Fount Paperbacks under the
title *Miracle on the River Kwai.*

First published in the United States by Zondervan in 2002.

Requests for information should be addressed to:
Zondervan, *Grand Rapids, Michigan 49530*

Ernest Gordon asserts the moral right to be identified as the author of this work.

A catalogue record for this book is available from the British Library.

ISBN 0 00 711848 1

All photos, except where noted, are courtesy of the Ernest Gordon Estate.

Printed in the United States of America

02 03 04 05 06 07 08 /DC/ 10 9 8 7 6 5 4 3 2 1

CONTENTS

INTRODUCTION

1 February 2000, Wampo, Thailand

It was a pleasant morning – not too hot. A brief downpour had left everything smelling sweet and fresh, and the ground was still steaming. My son Alastair and I had arrived the previous night after a flight from New York and a long drive north from Bangkok. We had come to Thailand to participate in the filming of a movie called *To End all Wars,* based on the story of this book. A section of the original rail line is still operational and we walked along a viaduct made of rough-hewn logs high above the river. We stopped for a rest in the cool shade of a cave and looked out over the bending Kwai Yai River. I was surprised to see how beautiful a river it was, with its steep cliffs and wild bamboo reaching into the muddy waters. The cave now serves as a local shrine and the golden statue of a Buddha sits serenely in the deepest recess.

Ironically, this area has become a popular tourist attraction. They come on package tours, take elephant rides along the river, watch native dances. Some come to lay wreaths at the war cemeteries in Chungkai and Kanchanaburi. Others come to visit a place that never really existed. They go in droves to Tamarkan and walk across the so-called 'Bridge on the River Kwai' because they have seen the great, if inaccurate, movie by British director David Lean. Historical fact and Hollywood fiction come together in a surreal mix. Sometimes it is hard to tell them apart. Once a year, there is even a *son et lumière* re-enactment of the bombing of the bridge by Allied bombers in June 1945 – all in a festive day's outing.

There were moments on this trip when the movie version of the River Kwai seemed more tangible than the 'real' story. It certainly felt odd to be here in a place that was still haunted by such human misery, with everything so pleasant and children selling slices of pineapple. A busload of tourists arrived in Wampo shortly after we got there. They stepped into the parking lot, took pictures of one another hanging over the ledge, bought postcards from a little souvenir hut. Some walked along the viaduct and peered into the cave where we were sitting, but they didn't stay long. As soon as a horn honked, they went scurrying back to their bus and headed off to another site.

I vaguely remembered the name of the place, Wampo, but at first I didn't recognize much about it. Then the landscape triggered a sequence of memories. There were two oddly shaped hills in the distance, almost like the stylized mountains you see in Chinese landscape paintings. I remembered the eccentric silhouettes of those hills, and then everything else fell into place. I had been here 58 years ago as a prisoner of war under the Japanese. I had lain here by the edge of the jungle; I had scrambled along this steep embankment, and waded into the muddy water where the river makes a double curve on its way south towards Kanchanaburi. I had worked with other Allied troops clearing back the jungle, helping to lay the railroad tracks that would eventually carry Japanese troops and supplies all the way to the Burma front. Today there are still a few clumps of bamboo growing here and there on the steeper hillsides, but most of the jungle has been cleared away.

Wampo was one of the first station stops on the Burma–Thailand railway, the infamous Railway of Death, so called because of the tragic toll it incurred. Its 415-kilometre route passed through dense rainforest and malarial swamps, over mountains and across rivers. We were exhausted, sick from tropical diseases and starvation, overworked, injured, dying off at a preposterous rate. Sixty thousand Allied prisoners of war were forced into slave labour as well as 270,000 Asian workers. More than 80,000 died during the railway's construction. That's approximately 393 lives lost for every mile of track laid – a hideous cost.

Now I recognize a spot just down the river – a sandy shoal that protruded into the current. That was where our camp had been set up when we worked on the viaduct. I also remembered the cave and how four of my fellow POWs had taken refuge there during an escape, but they were rounded up by Japanese guards and dragged back to the camp. During morning roll call the men were tied to posts and executed by a firing squad. An officer fired his pistol into the backs of their heads just to make sure they were dead. I remembered the sound of the four shots. It was a sickening spectacle intended to serve as a warning: anyone attempting to escape would be executed.

A few days later we arrived at the Kanchanaburi War Cemetery in a mini-van. The movie crew were busy setting up their equipment. Production assistants were hurrying around, placing reflectors and adjusting the boom microphones. It was already hot – one of the hottest days of our trip. The director, a young man in a baseball cap, was finally ready for the shot. I was told to walk through the marble arch of the entry gate and come forward at a leisurely place towards the middle of the cemetery to meet Nagase Takashi, a former Japanese officer who served as an interpreter in the camps along the Burma–Thailand railroad.

I walk forward. Mr Nagase shakes my hand and makes a formal apology for the atrocities committed by his fellow Japanese. I acknowledge his apology and then we walk together to the soldiers' monument at the far end of the cemetery, where we lay a wreath of flowers. We are asked to do this several times. The shot is not quite right. Mr Nagase isn't speaking loudly enough. I am standing in the wrong place. We do it again – my approach, the handshake, his apology, my acknowledgement, smiles, bows, etc. – repeating ourselves for the camera. It is getting hotter and the midday sun is beating down, making us all a bit queasy. Assistants run out after each shot to hold umbrellas over our heads and give us bottles of spring water.

To be sure, the moment was orchestrated, but the emotions were real. I was overcome by the sense of loss, the hatred, the senseless brutality of those years. Here in this tranquil place of manicured lawns and flowering shade trees, we walked past row after row of small headstones marking the remains of 6,982 Allied soldiers. So many brave men lost. I read some of their names out loud. There were young Scottish soldiers I had known as a captain in the Argyll and Sutherland Highlanders, and so many others: English, Australian, Dutch, men who would be in their eighties now, just like me. I thought of the ones who helped to lessen the suffering of others, the ones who guided me through my own time of suffering, the ones I describe in this book. My experience in the POW camps of Thailand changed my life. I survived where so many others died, but not a day has passed when I have not thought about them, my comrades, my friends, the ones who were left behind in this tropical land.

We all find ways to live with the past, to make peace and find our own reasons for carrying on. I wrote this book as a way of coming to terms with an impossible truth.

Ernest Gordon
Alastair Gordon
23 April 2001

And an highway shall be there, and a way, and it shall be called the way of holiness; the unclean shall not pass over it; but it shall be for those: the wayfaring men, though fools, shall not err therein.

Isaiah 35:8

IN MEMORY OF ERNEST GORDON

On 16 January 2002, after a long illness, my father, Ernest Gordon, died. He was remarkably tough and resilient – the consummate survivor who cheated death several times. But the last few months were difficult ones. He was hospitalized for a collapsed lung and other complications that even he couldn't overcome.

My father's message and mission could be summed up in the word *fellowship,* a concept that guided him throughout his life. During his three-and-a-half years of captivity in the POW camps of southeast Asia, he learned the hardest lesson of all: to forgive – and even love – one's enemies. These weren't allegorical opponents from biblical times, but modern men of the twentieth century. While so many of his comrades were consumed by anger, he discovered a sustaining belief in God and the capacity for love – even in a death camp. 'Selfishness, hatred, jealousy, and greed were all anti-life,' he later wrote. 'Love, self-sacrifice, mercy, and creative faith, on the other hand, were the essence of life, turning mere existence into living in its truest sense. These were the gifts of God to men.'

After his conversion in the camps, my father had a clear mission. He learned to shape his painful experiences into a narrative structure, first telling parts of his story in articles, lectures and sermons, then finally the whole account in this book. When first published in the United States by Harper & Row (1963) it was called *Through the Valley of the Kwai.* A year later it was published in Great Britain by William Collins as *Miracle on the River Kwai.* Now, in conjunction with the film, it is called *To End All Wars.*

But whatever the book's title, the significance of its content remains unchanged. And in today's global climate, its message seems more relevant than ever as it shows the need for tolerance, forgiveness and the possibility of reconciliation in a world fractured by hatred and war.

Alastair Gordon
21 February 2002

1

THE DEATH HOUSE

I was dreaming, and I was happy with my dreams. Within myself I heard the raucous cry of sea-gulls circling above the fishing-boats as the fishermen sorted their catch. I felt the touch of a salt-laden wind upon my face; I smelled the clean freshness of old-fashioned carbolic soap; I tasted the sweet bitterness of heavy Scottish ale.

I sensed the many things that were calling me to remembered life. Voluptuously, in my dreams, I was savouring the cosy luxury of freshly ironed sheets on my bed at home, and the friendly flicker of warm shadows that my bedroom fire cast upon the wall.

In the bewildering no-man's-land between the *was* and the *is* the pictures began to fade; the snug comfort evaporated; the crisp, clean smells of wholesomeness were engulfed. My waking senses, dragged reluctantly from their drowsing rest, experienced anew the smells of my existence as a prisoner of war of the Japanese in the jungles of Thailand. These were the corrupt smells of dying things – of decaying flesh, of rotting men.

Turning my head in the direction of the sound that had plucked me back to consciousness, I saw a small light lurching and staggering as if carried over uneven ground. I heard strained breathing and the irregular thud of bare feet on bare earth. Two British medical orderlies reached my end of the Death House with a body on a crude stretcher swaying between them in unsteady rhythm.

'Here you are, chum,' said the first orderly, as they dropped their load upon the ground. 'Another one to keep you company.'

The yellow flicker of the makeshift lamp gave just enough light for me to make out my comrades of the night. They were ten dead men wrapped in shrouds of straw rice-sacks. It was hard to tell that they were corpses. They might have been sacks of old rags or bones. The uncertain light and the prone position from which I was looking at them made them seem longer and heavier and more important than they were at other times to me. Even had they been plainly discernible as human carcasses – forms emptied of their humanity – I would not have minded. Corpses were as common amongst us as empty bellies.

I was lying at the morgue end of the Death House. Being on slightly higher and therefore less muddy terrain, this end was the most desirable section of the long, slummy bamboo hut which was supposed to be a hospital but had long since given up any pretence of being a place to shelter the sick. It was a place where men came to die.

'I hope no more shuffle off tonight,' I whispered.

'Don't worry,' said the orderly. 'This is probably the last. There are a couple of RCs on the edge, but like as not they'll hang on till morning. The priest gave them absolution last night, so they're all right. You know what they call that priest?'

I shook my head.

'The Angel of Death. Every time they see him come in the RCs wonder which of 'em is due to go. Some of the chaps don't mind knowing, but the others can't take it. "Nothing much you can do about it," I tells 'em. "The padre's got his job to do, and I dare say he doesn't like it any more than you do." Cor, I bet he was never half so busy in Blighty. If he was paid a quid for every one he sees off he'd be a bleedin' millionaire.'

As he talked, he and his companion rolled the corpse on to the ground and began to fit two rice-sacks over it.

'How old was he?' I asked.

'Oh, about twenty-one,' the first orderly replied. 'A Service Corps bloke with the 18th Division. Only came to Chungkai about five days ago.'

They performed their task with the deftness of old hands, pulling one sack over the head and the other over the feet. While they were pulling up the lower sack, the left hand flopped over on the ground. As it lay there, uselessly, helplessly, it seemed the most significant dead thing about the body. Curious how dead it looked. It was good for nothing. It would never work again, nor be raised in protest, nor point to something exciting, nor touch another gently. Its stillness seemed to shout, 'This is death!'

The hand was stuffed into the top sack, both sacks were tied together with pieces of atap grass, and the body was stacked with others about two feet from where I lay.

'Might as well take a breather,' said the first orderly.

'It's been a long night,' observed the other. They sat down beside me. For a few moments there was silence.

'The only ambition I've got,' said the first one, reflectively, 'is to die of old age. Cor, it would be great to have a family – a couple of sons, say. Watch them grow up; then, when you've had your life, see them come round to keep you company. That'd be a bit of all right, that would.'

He sighed.

'All this here death is so pointless – because it's at the wrong time. It's so bloody stupid – death for nothing. The time's been mucked up. A man ought to have a bit of dignity for himself, even when he's dead. But that's just what we haven't got.'

'Our trouble is,' said his mate, 'we were born at the wrong time and in the wrong country.'

They were silent again for a moment, then rose and picked up the stretcher, ready once more to play their part as hosts in the House of the Dead. As their lamp receded down the hut, darkness shrouded me again. I was now so thoroughly awake that I couldn't get back to sleep. I resented this, for sleep was the most precious thing I could experience. It wasn't that I minded lying on the ground, for my body had practically no feeling left in it. Since nature had anaesthetized it, why couldn't it have done the same thing with my mind and granted me peace?

I could not say, as Odysseus did, 'Be strong, my heart; ere now worse fate was thine' – it was hard to imagine a worse fate. However, I could say, as Achilles did to Odysseus in Hades, 'Don't say a word in favour of death; rather would I be a slave in a pauper's home and be above ground than be a king of kings among the dead.'

To all intents the advantage was still mine. I was alive. I could think. I existed.

The dawn came suddenly and harshly, bringing with it stifling heat, stark light and sharp shadows. The hut looked more like a Death House than ever – filthy, squalid and desolate. Through the gaps in the atap walls I could see open latrines, and beyond them bamboos touching bamboos in an infinite pattern that stretched out for a thousand miles to where freedom lay – and also reached in to hold us fast in a green prison.

Yes, I knew where I was; I was in a prison camp by the River Kwai. I knew who I was; I was a company commander in the 93rd Highlanders. And yet I wasn't. I was a prisoner of war, a man lying with the dead, waiting for them to be carried away so that I might have more room.

Ruffling my black beard, I wondered why I had had to end up in such a place. What a contrast this was to the way in which my ill-starred odyssey had begun – a beginning associated in my mind with summer in a civilized, or comparatively civilized world.

It was a good summer, that one of 1939. I had hastened back from the University of St Andrews to my home on the Firth of Clyde in time to take part in an ocean race to the south of Ireland and back on the old Clyde Forty *Vagrant*. The summer had had a stormy beginning, for a nor'-easter dispersed the fleet on the homeward leg and we had to limp into Dublin for repairs, although we finished third out of a large fleet. But from then on the season was a series of gay regattas and long, happy cruises. Skies were blue; winds were fair and warm. The Firth was saturated with beauty. Each day, each event, each incident, seemed more delightful than the one before. I had very little money, but I lived like a millionaire on what small skill I had as a yachtsman.

In July I skippered a yacht on a cruise up the west coast of Scotland, seeking harbour by night in lochs protected by hills ancient with wisdom and offering a rare serenity to those ready to accept it. That cruise over, I sailed from Sandbank to Cowes in my favourite yacht, the *Dione*. It was a 'couthy' sail, the whole seven hundred miles of it. My crew mates had a hearty lust for life; the four of us were on a spree, conscious perhaps, with war looming up, that we had to make the most of all that was joyous, clean and open-hearted. Although I sailed so continuously, there was always time for a girl in most ports. The more interesting the girl, the more favoured the port.

There was an ominous undertone, however, to the gaiety of that summer. Possibly my foreboding came from a feeling that I was living on borrowed time. I'd had a spell of duty in the Royal Air Force, which ended with an accident that left me with a fractured skull and spine. While recovering, I sensed that the drums of war were already sounding, so before going to battle I went to the university to read history and philosophy, more for my own enjoyment than for anything else.

My disablement had gained me a pleasant respite from the profession of arms. The future was so uncertain that I did not worry much about preparing for any other career. In my own leisurely fashion I was bent on savouring the delight of living. Today was mine; tomorrow could wait.

Fair winds and stately yachts, good companions and bonnie lassies, laughing days and carefree nights, seldom last as long as we would like. So busy had I been pursuing my favourite sport that I had paid no attention to what was happening on the international scene.

On 23 August, while I was taking part in an inter-varsity regatta, Germany signed a non-aggression pact with the Soviet Union. I did not learn this until I returned to my lodgings in Clynder, at the close of the day's racing, to find a telegram for me lying on the hall table. It was from my parents, telling me that my brother had been called up in the Royal Engineers and suggesting that it was time I returned home. The halcyon days were over. A long, fearsome struggle confronted us all.

I had made up my mind that I wouldn't spend the war 'flying a desk'. If I couldn't fight in the air I would fight on the ground. On my return home, I telephoned the secretary of our local Territorial Association in Dunoon to ask if there were any vacancies for commissions in the Argyll and Sutherland Highlanders. I was told that there were and if I rushed over I could have one fairly quickly.

I lost no time, and was posted first to one of the Territorial battalions and then, after a month or so, to the 2nd Battalion – the 93rd Highlanders. This battalion, a proud body with a noble tradition, originated during the Napoleonic Wars when Major General Wemyss raised a regiment in the county of Sutherland in the north-east corner of Scotland. Those he tried to recruit were so independent that at first they refused to accept the king's shilling. They came round eventually when they were allowed to serve under fellow Highlanders rather than English officers and to take their own kirk to war with them as part of the regiment.

After the Battle of Balaclava the battalion became known as the 'Thin Red Line', because it had halted the Russian cavalry charge. In the reign of Queen Victoria it was united with the 91st or Argyllshire Highlanders to form the Argyll and Sutherland Highlanders. The 93rd made up the 2nd Battalion, and at the outbreak of the First World War the regiment was the first to land in France and the first to see action.

Although we were a Highland regiment, most of the officers came from south of the Highland Fault Line or south of the border. Our Jocks came from the industrial belt stretching between the Forth and Clyde rivers; from Edinburgh, Falkirk, Motherwell, Hamilton, Clydebank, Greenock, Gourock, Port Glasgow and Stirling.

They were in the Army for a variety of reasons: because they had imbibed tales of martial glory with their mothers' milk and so soldiering was in their blood; because the glamour of a soldier's uniform offered a cheerful contrast to the squalor of the slums from which they had come; because it was a way of earning a living; or simply because they were running away from a past.

After I was mobilized I visited St Andrews to retrieve some books and see friends. I went straight to the bar of the Imperial Hotel, a popular students' haunt, to show off my fine new uniform with its bright Glengarry bonnet, its badger's-head sporran and its green-and-blue kilt. The bar was almost deserted except for a travelling salesman and a fellow student, of pronounced Marxist views. The student lounging against the bar, looked me up and down.

'What the hell are you doing in that rig-out? Don't you

know it'll be all over by Christmas? You're just wasting your own time and the taxpayers' money.'

His remark came as something of a shock. But it was to take many shocks to shake us from our complacent belief that all would soon be back to normal.

In early November I was given a week's embarkation leave, my first and last in what was to be a long war. This was a disappointing experience. It rained all the time. I went around to say goodbye, but the men I knew were already scattered. I had hoped to receive a hero's farewell from my girl friends. But they, too, had gone to serve king and country in one or other of the services. I slept for the last time in the comfort of my own bed, bade a sad farewell to my parents, my sister Grace and my brother Pete, and caught the train for regimental headquarters at Stirling Castle.

To the north of Glasgow, half-way between the Rivers Clyde and Forth, the castle stands with its turrets thrust aggressively skyward, as though conscious of its role as sentinel on the route to the Highlands. On a misty grey Saturday afternoon in the late autumn of 1939 I paraded on the square with a small detachment of first-line reinforcements. At the far end stood a knot of newly arrived recruits, eyeing us with awe. They were very conscious that we were soldiers – already on our way to war.

The orderly sergeant of the day took the roll-call of my men, and handed them over to me as 'all present and correct'. Hurriedly I inspected them and gave the order to slope arms. With a 'right turn' and a 'quick march', we were off. The sentry at the main gate came to attention, and presented arms in salute as we marched from that high, stark fastness.

There is only one way out of Stirling Castle, and that is down. Downhill we marched, down the steep brae, past the Castle Inn where the 'other ranks' drank their beer, down past the Red Lion where the officers sipped their whisky, down the main cobbled street that led to the railway station.

The scene in Stirling was like that on any other Saturday. Housewives dragged reluctant husbands along – or left them standing while they paused to gossip with passing friends – standing and thinking wistfully of the soccer games they might have been following on the wireless. They paid no attention to us as we marched by. This was not yet the day of the soldier.

Downward our way continued – all the way down the world; down through England; down through France by stages; down through the Red Sea and the Indian Ocean by troopship; down through the dripping jungle of Malaya on foot; down through the mud and the blood in the heart-breaking retreat to the last stand in Singapore; until all that was left of our thousand-strong battalion was a battered remnant of one hundred and twenty.

In keeping with the regimental tradition of being first in action and last out, the Argylls were the last troops to cross from the Malayan mainland to Singapore Island. We sauntered over the Causeway while our last two pipers played 'Highland Laddie', the regimental march. Also in line with our tradition, the battalion commanding officer, Lt Colonel Iain Stewart, his batman and myself as rear company commander were the last across. No sooner had we set foot on the island than the Causeway was blown up behind us to seal in Singapore's inhabitants on 30 December 1942.

On down through the island our remnant fought – until only thirty were left – until the defending forces ran out of drinking water, ammunition, land and hope. And even after that my own way continued, down across the Straits to Sumatra, by commandeered ferry. It came to a halt in a coastal city called Padang.

2

SOLDIERS AT SEA

The last British warship taking off refugees had sailed from Padang a few days before I got there. The whole of Sumatra was about to fall. I knew that I must plan a way of escape, and that I'd have to do it at once if I was to do it at all, for the enemy was already closing in on the city. Australia, India and Ceylon were the nearest countries free from Japanese domination. But they were all a long way from Sumatra.

I was walking down the main street one morning, pondering ways and means, when a familiar voice hailed me. I turned to encounter a colonel of the India Army Service Corps whom I recognized at once. He was one of those whom two fellow officers and I had passed through the escape route we had been operating from Tambilihan on the Indragiri River on Sumatra's east coast.

'I thought you'd be on your way to India by this time,' I said as we shook hands, 'on board one of those cruisers that picked up the last loads.'

He shrugged fatalistically.

'No such luck. I followed your example and stayed to organize a transit camp a little upriver from you. I got into Padang two days before you did. I heard you were here and I've been hunting for you ever since. May I have a word with you?'

'Certainly,' I said, curious to know what he had on his mind.

He led the way to a coffee-house with a few iron tables set out on the street under a canopy. Two Malays in black sunkas (brimless caps), white bajus (open-necked shirts) and bright sarongs were paying their chits and getting up to leave.

The waiter brought us our coffee. When he had moved away the colonel said to me in a matter-of-fact voice, 'I'm forming an official escape party. Would you care to join it?'

I stared at him dumbfounded.

'Of course I would! What's the plan?'

He leaned closer across the table.

'One of the last messages we received from General Wavell's HQ said that if no help arrives an attempt to escape should be made by a group of officers. And it's very unlikely now that any help is going to get through to us before the Japs take over.'

I nodded. 'I agree. Worse luck.'

'As senior officer here, it's my responsibility to see that the order is carried out. I've been in touch with the Netherlands Government chaps in Padang. They say they don't want to do anything official – if the Japs found out they'd take it out on them.'

'What exactly is your scheme, then?' I said, trying to curb my impatience. But he was determined to come to the point in his own way.

'Unofficially, however, the Dutch have given me some money; they say it's none of their business what I do with it. They've also loaned me two cars, to be returned when I've finished with them – and no questions asked. I'm told there's a chance we may be able to buy a sailing-boat at a fishing village called Sasok, about a hundred miles north of here.'

It sounded too good to be true. I must have betrayed my incredulity.

'Well,' he said, 'it won't be quite what you're used to at the Royal Singapore Yacht Club. But she'd have sail – and she'd float. The south-west monsoon's due to break in May. With a bit of luck we may get the benefit of its winds a little earlier than that and make Ceylon comfortably.'

'It's possible,' I said, 'Ceylon can't be more than twelve hundred miles away.'

The colonel frowned. 'But it won't be all that easy – not with the Jap Navy and Air Force all over the Indian Ocean.'

'Who are going?' I asked.

'I've worked out a list of nine. You may know some of them. There are three navy types: Crawley – remember him? He sailed up to HQ in Tambilihan in a junk. And two from the Royal Malayan Naval Reserve. Then there's a major from the Sappers and a captain from the Signals. Including myself – and you – that'll be ten altogether.'

'Could you take two more?' I asked. 'I'd like Rigden and MacLaren to come along. They were with me on the escape boat.'

He shook his head.

'Sorry, old boy. I'm afraid it just isn't possible. Rigden has been assigned as dockmaster, you know, in case a warship should come in. And MacLaren has been put in charge of the troops as sergeant-major.'

I felt that I was letting my friends down. 'Are you sure we can't change that?' I pleaded.

'Absolutely. We've got to get cracking. Besides, we'd be doing them a pretty doubtful favour. This will be a risky business. If we're caught we'll almost certainly be executed.'

This eased my conscience somewhat.

'When do we leave for Sasok?'

'At dawn, day after tomorrow.'

'Anything I can do meanwhile?'

'Don't think so, thank you. I've got the Malayan Volunteers picking up as many tins of food as they can find. The New Zealand naval officer is out hunting up navigational instruments and a book of nautical tables. The sapper is putting together a first-aid box – and I think that's about it.' Then he added, 'I'll tell you what, though. You might invest in some cigarettes. They'd come in handy as barter.'

'Right. Now what about clothing?'

'Take what you've got. I dare say it isn't much.'

'What I have on – plus a spare pair of shorts, a shirt and a tooth-brush. What about weapons? I know where I can put my hands on some sub-machineguns.'

'No, I don't think that would be a good idea. We'll be dealing with natives, and it might put the wind up them if they saw us armed to the teeth. Take your side-arms, that's all.'

The colonel drained his last drop of coffee, lighted a cigarette and lounged back comfortably in his chair. He was ready for chit-chat.

'Tell me,' he said, 'how did you get away from Singapore?'

'Someone at Command conceived the brilliant notion of running a ferry service between Malaya and Singapore to bring in supplies. I was to be in charge. But, of course, it never began operations because it was based on the erroneous assumption that Singapore would hold out indefinitely.'

'What happened then?'

'As you know, everything was in a state of utter confusion after the collapse. On Friday morning – that was the Black Friday of 13 February – I was ordered to go to one of the islands off Changi that was garrisoned by the Second Dogras. I was to take them off on ferry-boats and then land them behind the Jap lines on the west sector of Singapore Island.'

'But it would have been about three days too late by then, surely?'

'It was. When I reached the Dogras' HQ I learned that the whole deal was off. The next morning I discovered that a ferry-boat had arrived the night before, commanded by Sergeant-Major MacLaren. I sent a signal to Command HQ telling them that I was on my way in the ferry. HQ replied that I was to proceed on my own. We made it back to Keppel

Harbour. As we were entering, a Jap battery shelled us, so we moved out into the Straits and lay there until Sunday.

'All that day we kept picking up boatloads of escapees. Around midnight we came across four men in a canoe. From them we learned that the show was over – had been over since eight-thirty that evening.

'That's about the time the CO sent his last message, saying that, because of losses from enemy action and the lack of supplies and ammunition, he could continue to fight no longer,' the colonel mused. 'It was the sign-off. Too bad I didn't bump into you then. I might have had a more comfortable trip.'

I laughed.

'Don't be too sure about that. I had no charts and I didn't know where the mine-fields were. But we got the ferry through somehow and sailed up the Indragiri to Rengat. There we found everything in a bonnie mess. I'd picked up Tom Rigden on the way over. When we heard about the nurses, women and children who were left behind on the islands we decided to stay and run an escape service for the ones who were stranded after the Japs attacked the last convoy from Singapore.'

'That was a bad business, wasn't it? I heard the whole convoy was sunk.'

'Yes, that's true. We picked up quite a few of the survivors. The nurses put up a terrific show.'

'Was there anyone at Rengat trying to organize things?'

'Oh yes, there was an Intelligence major named Campbell who was doing his best. He suggested that I should go back to Tambilihan and run things from there. As a matter of fact, he gave me this chit. He had the idea that we could get cooperation from the Dutch and put together some kind of resistance movement.'

I produced a slip from my wallet and read from it: 'This is to say that Captain Ernest Gordon of the Argyll and Sutherland Highlanders is empowered to act on behalf of His Majesty's

Government. Any assistance given to him in the form of money, arms or equipment will be paid for at a later date. All bills incurred by him as military representative in Sumatra will be honoured.'

A gleam lit up the colonel's eyes.

'Keep that!' he exclaimed. 'It may be very useful.'

I folded the chit carefully and returned it to my wallet. It did not occur to me that, far from proving useful, it might put my life in jeopardy.

The colonel pushed back his chair and looked at his watch.

'About time I moved along,' he said. 'I'm meeting the British Acting Vice-Consul at noon.'

He lowered his voice.

'Morning after next. Be outside the school by 0500 hours. No later. Goodbye.'

The first suggestion of dawn was paling the sky behind the palm trees as shadowy figures began to materialize in the school-yard. Introductions were brief. The borrowed cars had been carefully packed the night before. With a minimum of fuss and delay we took our places.

The colours of the buildings around us were beginning to show as the wheels crunched on the gravel of the driveway, and we set off, heading north for Sasok.

'It's a long haul to freedom,' I thought to myself as I listened to the music of the wheels on the road. 'But at least we're on our way.'

At Fort De Kock we encountered the headquarters of the Dutch forces. The officers informed us that the Japanese were advancing rapidly, and that to proceed farther would mean certain capture. We chose to take that chance.

When we passed their forward positions we began to appreciate the wisdom of their advice. We crossed a bridge. A few minutes later we heard a muffled *boom*. It had just blown up. At the first opportunity we turned off the main highway on to a single-track road that wound and twisted up into the hills. We were in the nick of time. From the top of the first rise we saw the dust of a Japanese column rising from the road we had just left.

The mountain track was breath-taking, coiling like a snake around steep hills, crossing roaring torrents on shaky bridges, and slipping through dark cavernous jungle until it left the hills behind and entered the low-lying coastal area. Before long we came upon a fair-sized village where the controller or district officer had his headquarters. He received us warmly, handed us a letter to his assistant at Sasok and sold us a welcome case of beer.

It was late afternoon when we reached Sasok, a fishing village at the mouth of a river. We were pleased to see two fairly sea-worthy-looking craft, of a Malay type called prahu, tied up along the bank. With the help of the assistant controller we opened negotiations with the natives, and finally bought a ship for two thousand dollars. From the smiles on the faces of the onlookers we judged that the Malays had had by far the best of the bargain.

Our purchase was named the *Setia Berganti*. She was about fifty feet overall and rather broad in the beam. Her deckhouse, thatched and canted like the roof of a hut, ran almost the length of the ship, leaving only a short deck space fore and aft. Her unusually long bowsprit, lending a rakish air, was her only saving grace. Her hull, however, appeared to be sound, and her bottom was copper-sheathed. She was not exactly a thing of grace and beauty, but she was our Argosy of fortune.

'Puts you in mind of Noah's Ark, doesn't it?'

A well-set-up man, with fair complexion and an easy manner, was standing by my side, looking the prahu over. He was Edward Hooper, former harbour-master of Singapore and member of the Royal Malayan Naval Reserve, who was to be our skipper. In his spotless white naval shorts and shirt, his white knee-length stockings and white shoes, he was the picture of smartness and efficiency. He seemed to have little in common with the dowdy craft.

The skipper identified a small kiosk on the port side of the fore-deck as the wood-burning galley, and a big box suspended overside from the starboard shrouds as the combined bathroom and head. The vessel had one drawback as far as comfort was concerned – she had no sleeping quarters. Her Malay crews, Hooper said, slept on the copra cargoes. I looked at her rig.

'Queer set-up,' I noted. 'It's a ketch, but I don't like the way the main boom runs abaft the mizzen. We'll need to top it up every time we go about. Heaven help us if we ever have an accidental jibe.'

'Wouldn't be the best thing to happen,' the skipper agreed. 'Perhaps we'd better have a closer look at the sails.'

We walked up the short gang-plank and went aboard. He fingered a fold of sail.

'Not much better than butter muslin.'

'A bit on the gossamer side,' I said. 'Think we'll ever get to Ceylon with those?'

'Touch and go,' the skipper replied. 'Perhaps you'd better scout around the shops and lay in a few bolts of cloth in case we have to make repairs. It'd be a good idea to get plenty of rope, too.'

By the time I returned with some bolts of cloth it was getting dark. The headman offered to let us spend the night in the one-room school, and we gladly accepted. But we were so excited at the prospect of escape that we had trouble in settling down for the night. We kept up a running cross-fire of conversation.

'Golly, these floors are hard,' moaned Limey, the British naval officer who was to be our cook. He had been badly hurt in the shoulder by a fragment of high explosive in the naval battle on Black Friday, and was threshing about trying to make himself comfortable.

'Not so hard as the floors in a Jap prison,' retorted Anzac, the New Zealand type. 'I'll take these any time. We're still free and we've got a chance of making a getaway. I wonder how those poor jokers in Singapore are making out.'

'Hard to tell, Anzac,' the Colonel sighed. 'There's been no word. But one thing you can be sure of – they're having no picnic.'

'You can say that again,' the skipper put in. 'If we set sail as quickly as possible we've a pretty good chance of not knowing what it's like being a prisoner of war.'

'And keep going at all costs,' said Limey. 'It's me for the girls and the high times in Ceylon. I'm sure to know some girls there. I know girls everywhere.'

'Stow the girls,' the Colonel growled. 'We've a tough job ahead tomorrow. We need our sleep.'

At dawn we were awakened by a babble of voices. Outside our quarters Malays were streaming in from all directions, laden with foodstuffs. They had come in response to our request. A regular market began to take shape, with baskets of limes, eggs, pineapples, sweet potatoes, yams, paw-paws, pomelos, dried fish and bananas spread out on the ground.

Limey attended to the victualling, while the rest of us carried out our assigned tasks. All that day we worked, loading ballast, stores and water, overhauling the rigging and splicing rope. Towards evening, order began to appear. With a grateful sigh, we lugged the last of our supplies aboard.

Our water was stored in six oil-drums of fifty-five-gallon capacity each, and ninety four-gallon petrol-cans open at the top. This gave us six hundred and ninety gallons, which we believed to be enough to last us for at least thirty days, even allowing for wastage.

Provisions, too, were reasonably adequate. We had two baskets of tinned goods and two full sacks of rice. We hardboiled a number of duck eggs and took along all the green fruit we could buy. In our pile of green coconuts we had an emergency reserve of both food and liquid. We stowed everything in the hold and covered it with the split bamboo to serve as a kind of deck.

That afternoon the village headman gave us a farewell party. A throng of children came to the prahu to escort us back to the village centre. Mountains of fried chicken and rice and fresh fruits were provided for us by the headman. One old man waved his arms up and down and blew lustily with his mouth, thus wishing us in pantomime a successful sea voyage.

Ralph Salmon, our interpreter, made a speech of thanks and farewell to which the headman replied with courteous formality: 'We are sorry that you cannot stay to enjoy our company. We have liked you. Now that you must leave us, we salute you and wish you good fortune on your long journey. May friendly winds take you quickly to your own people, and away from your enemy, the Japanese. When the war is over, and you have defeated them, come back to see us and we shall have another feast.'

Blessings and good wishes were lavished on us all the way to the prahu. The former crew insisted on coming aboard and setting the sails for us. Then they cast off and began poling us across the bar. The four Malay sailors were a picturesque sight as they worked silhouetted against the last light of day, swinging their poles in rhythm to a weird melody of quartertones. Full ahead the sun in all its fiery glory was descending into the sea.

The skipper and I were lounging by the deckhouse, relishing the fresh evening breeze.

'This would be a bit of all right – if we didn't have the Japs breathing down our necks,' the skipper said.

I nodded.

He glanced down at the Malays.

'I'll bet you never started on an ocean race like this before.'

'I'll tell you this,' I replied. 'I never set out on one where the stakes were so high.'

The skipper's tanned face was serious.

'Yes – freedom and our lives – those are high stakes, all right.'

A little way down the deck, Limey was leaning his elbows on the rail. Suddenly he began to recite:

> *Sunset and evening star*
> *And one clear call for me:*
> *May there be no moaning at the bar*
> *When I put out to sea.*

'He's thinking of all those unpaid chits at Raffles bar in Singapore,' said Anzac with a grin.

'I'll bet he left a few of those behind,' the skipper chuckled.

There was a burst of laughter. The tension, which had been building up with our departure, eased.

We were over the bar now. The Malays lifted their poles, lashed them to the side of the deckhouse, and climbed over the rail to their dug-out canoe which the prahu had been towing behind. They cast off and stood up, bidding us farewell in an elaborate pantomime that combined good wishes with sharp sallies.

'Whoever heard of soldiers sailing their own boat?' their gestures seemed to say. 'Now you have only wind and water to fight. But since you must fight them – fight well!'

Quickly it became night. A gentle zephyr eased us out to sea. We were on our way.

At the tiller, the skipper puffed silently at his pipe and gazed contentedly over the Indian Ocean. After a time he called us together to set the shipboard routine. To Anzac, also a master mariner, he gave responsibility for the navigation. I was to be second mate. The colonel and Ralph Salmon were assigned to my watch. The skipper was to have the first watch, I the middle watch and Anzac the morning watch. Since Limey was not fit for heavier work, he was made paymaster and cook.

The skipper looked me over, taking stock of my large frame and ruddy Scottish complexion.

'You're a healthy-looking type,' he said. 'I'm going to call you Rosie.'

In the chaotic conditions that followed the fall of Singapore men from all the services, from all the nations of the Commonwealth, were thrown together for a brief time and then parted. We seldom knew a man's full name. We gave one another generic nicknames and the nicknames stuck. A Londoner was given the tag of 'Limey'; an Australian was known as 'Aussie'; and so on. Thus I became known as 'Rosie'.

Soon a singing wind came from the east, speeding us on our course. When I was called at midnight to take my watch I found that the wind had increased. We were making a good seven knots. No moon shone, but the silver brilliance of the stars lighted the white foam of the waves to a glow. The quietness around us was so different from the abrupt silence which had come sometimes in the midst of battle. It was the quietness of a pleasing symphony – a symphony of wind and waves and water gurgling in friendly fashion along the humming hull.

All went well through the next day. But the following dawn our kindly wind left us and we were at the mercy of an awkward sea. Sharp puffs came from every quarter, only to die down again.

It was my watch below, but I could not sleep. In the hold every sound from above deck was greatly amplified – the flap of the sails, the crack of booms, the rattle of the blocks. Suddenly there was a steep, heavy lurch. With it came the heart-breaking sound of canvas ripping. On deck all was chaos.

The accidental jibe I had dreaded had taken place. In the course of it the mainsail had been caught by the mizzen, and it was rent from head to foot, clew to throat, leech to luff. In place of the bellying sail that had been hurrying us along, a pitiful bundle of shreds hung lifeless from the mainmast.

No one spoke, but each one thought, 'Does this mean that we're not going to make it?' Everyone put on a good face, however, and gathered in the tatters. All was not quite lost. The jib, staysail and mizzen were still set. To these we added a spare jib which we set on the mainmast.

Throughout the day, while we sailed slowly under our sparse canvas, we sewed furiously, hard put to it to keep our balance as we wallowed in a heavy sea. With the patience of despair, we pieced together a jigsaw from the rags that remained. At last we hoisted it, hardly daring to breathe. It held together. We allowed ourselves a faint cheer.

Later that night the wind steadied and freshened enough to take us along at four knots. We were on the move again, conscious that every mile of our wake meant a mile nearer safety.

About half-way through my watch I thought I saw something. My eyes were tired, so I rubbed them to make sure. No doubt about it. Two islands were coming up fast on the starboard bow.

The presence of any islands was enough to make us uneasy. They were likely to be coral reefs, whose sharp teeth could chew into our hull. We had no charts of these waters. Our navigational aids, on a par with those of early sailing-ship days, consisted of a compass, a school atlas in Dutch (which none of us could read) and a naval book of nautical tables. We calculated our position daily by means of our day's work. That is, we averaged our course, distance and leeway, and worked out our position with the aid of the log tables. At any given date we knew only roughly where we were.

The islands passed by to starboard. I could hear the soughing of the waves embracing them.

My watch came to an end, and, still worried about our position, I turned in. I had hardly dropped off to sleep when the thump of running feet jerked me awake. What alarmed me more than the sound of the crew was the noise of booming surf smashing against a lee shore. I rushed on deck and through the pitch dark made out a mass of frothing foam, much too near us. Then I heard two splashes. The men on watch had let go both anchors and were paying out the hawsers. I joined in. We made them fast to the bits and waited. The anchors held. We were safe for the time being.

Within an hour dawn came. Our pulses slowed at what it disclosed. On all sides of us waves were breaking into white bubbles over atolls and coral reefs. But we were afloat and in calm waters. Miraculously, we had sailed into a lagoon. As the day strengthened, a beautiful scene emerged from the darkness: a succession of green, palm-fringed islands bordered with white beaches rose from the emerald-and-sapphire sea.

We lowered over the side the eleven-foot dug-out canoe lashed to the foredeck for just such an emergency. The Colonel, Salmon and I got in, and paddled along the lagoon until we came to an inlet where we could see a cluster of palm-leaf huts. Beaching the canoe, we went ashore to meet a large family of what appeared to be fisherfolk who had come out to greet us. Through Salmon we learned that we were on an island called Pini. This was only a small settlement, however; the head village was four or five miles away. The skipper decided that I should take Salmon and go to ask the headman's help in getting us out of the lagoon. Two of the fishermen volunteered to paddle us over.

One of them, a memorable character who was a kind of patriarch, had only one eye. We nicknamed him Nelson. He used his empty socket with devastating effect, turning it full upon us whenever he questioned our intelligence, which was often. Age, sun and sea had made his face a thing of wrinkled splendour. A permanent leering grin rounded off his character, giving him a lusty, villainous mien. While we paddled, I struck up a conversation with him through Salmon.

'Have you lived here most of your life?'

'All of my life, naturally.'

'What do you do?'

'I fish. What else would I do?'

'Do you like working at sea'

'Oh yes. I know all about the sea. I understand it. I can get fish from it. We get on well together.'

He bobbed his head and screwed up his one good eye wisely as he said this.

'Foolish man,' he seemed to be implying. 'Can't you see I know my trade? See how I paddle this canoe! See how I can tell the ways of the water! The ocean and I are one!'

After crossing a brilliant blue bay we could see the village. The headman was already moving gracefully down the beach towards us. His white baju and sarong blended with the glistening sand, white in the sunlight, so that he seemed only face and arms and legs and feet. We shook hands without ceremony, in an act of friendship.

'Come to my hut,' he said, 'and I will refresh you.'

The hut was spacious and clean, with the few furnishings neatly in order. The headman's wife brought us clear coffee in glasses and a basket of small sweet bananas. We were describing our predicament when she returned, bearing a delicious meal of fried chicken, fried fish, steaming rice and a tray of empty bowls.

This was an enchanting interlude. Our host and hostess treated us with friendly courtesy, anticipating our every want. We made no attempt to hurry our conversation. We told them about the war, how we were escaping from the Japanese, how we had ripped our mainsail, repaired it as best we could and how we had miraculously found our way through the reefs into the placid waters of the lagoon.

'What we need most of all at this moment is sails, rope and a pilot,' I told the headman.

'I cannot give you rope or sails,' he said, 'but I shall be delighted to pilot you to Tana Masa, another larger island about forty miles to the north-east. There you will be able to buy rope and other gear.'

'You are very kind,' I exclaimed. 'I am afraid we are causing you a great deal of trouble.'

'Not at all,' replied the headman graciously, 'your troubles are my troubles.'

When we got back to our base, at the edge of the lagoon we found it a scene of frenzied activity. A furious sewing bee was in progress. Eight fishermen were seated with our crew-mates in a circle on the sand, white and tanned arms going vigorously. They had pegged out on the ground the bolts of cloth I had bought in Sasok and were stitching them together into a sail. We dropped on the sand beside them and joined in.

Darkness fell. Someone fetched a lantern from the prahu and we worked on by its light, with stiff fingers, aching muscles and strained eyes. It was almost midnight when we finished.

We passed our cigarettes among the fishermen. 'Tailor-mades' did not often come their way and they were voluble in their thanks. We all lay down to rest on the beach. It seemed I had just dropped off when I felt a tap on my shoulder. I roused myself to see Nelson's baleful socket glaring down on me. He had come before dawn to volunteer to go with us to Tana Masa as our sailing master.

Speedily we bent on the new mainsail and stowed the repaired one as a spare. The first light of the new day was just edging the sky when off to starboard we saw the headman's outrigger ghosting towards us in an air so light we could hardly feel it. In a moment the headman himself hailed us. 'I've come to pilot you to Tana Masa. Follow me when you are ready. Perhaps there will be wind when the sun rises.'

We set sail and weighed anchor, but we did not move. No puff of wind could we find anywhere. Finally there came a breath that nudged the prahu, just enough to permit us to follow the headman's outrigger.

I stood with Limey at the after-rail, enjoying the calm beauty around us. We looked down into the water. It was crystal-clear and sparkling blue – a bluer blue than I had seen anywhere. Turrets and minarets of every colour formed fascinating coral cities through which schools of well-fed fish patrolled at leisure.

The clamour of war seemed far away. Island after island passed our beam as we drifted gently along. Coconut palms fringing the coral shores suggested cool breezes and a life of gracious ease. It was all very tempting. The waters swarmed with fish and the islands abounded with tasty fruits of a wide variety. Why bother to struggle on? Why not bribe the natives with our remaining cigarettes to build us one of their palm-leaf huts and live on here among these kind and generous people until the war was over?

I told Limey of my thoughts.

'How about it?' he said, winking at me. 'If we do reach Ceylon you know darned well we'll be pushed into some bloody mess or other the minute we get there. Why not stay and be lords of these islands? We'll fish and hunt like gentlemen, and in our spare time we'll brew coconut brandy. Then we'll settle back in our hammocks in our palm-leaf palaces and wait for lovely dusky princesses to come courting us!'

The Colonel was listening, farther down the rail.

'Wouldn't that be the life!' he exclaimed. 'And we'd go on from island to island. Just think – we could win an empire by living, while everyone else is losing theirs – by dying!'

The skipper joined in: 'By gum, we could train monkeys to be our servants! Intelligent little buggers, they are, you know.'

Limey's fancy began to take flight.

'We could rig up a big fan. Have them pull it with their tails, as they swing to and fro. While we lie there on our soft beds with our mouths open, waiting for the ripe fruit to drop in, they'll be working like nailers to keep us cool!'

Suddenly the skipper straightened up and peered towards the horizon.

'What's that?' he exclaimed.

Squinting our eyes, we could just make out a dark speck. It might be enemy. On the other hand, it might be a friendly ship.

'It's too far off – they'll never see us,' said Limey.

'Oh, I don't know about that,' said Anzac. 'Here, I've got a mirror. Try signalling with it, Skipper.'

Kneeling on the deck, the skipper began to flash signals. We waited. The sun flashed back signals of its own on the sparkling water. Our eyes, however, were well enough trained by now to distinguish between the fancied and the real; no signal was coming from the ship.

The smudge had gone. Long after there was nothing to see, the skipper kept on signalling. At last he gave up. He leaned down and rested the mirror against the rail. When he straightened up to stretch himself he kicked it accidentally with his foot. It fell forward. He knelt to pick it up; it was broken in two.

'Now see what you've done,' wailed Limey. 'Seven years' bad luck for all of us – that's what it is! You've broken the bloody thing!'

We stared at the glittering pieces. We knew we were not superstitious. Luck was what you did with what you had. It was what you made for yourself – by yourself – for good or ill. And yet . . .

Anzac was a steady type. 'Well, it isn't as though it's been smashed to smithereens, you know. It's only broken in two,' he said in his cool, slow voice. 'That's only three and a half years' bad luck. Maybe they're the ones we've just had. You wouldn't exactly call Singapore lucky, would you?'

The tension eased. Anzac picked up the pieces and took them below.

While we were waiting for the wind to freshen, we fished. We had only bent pins for hooks and balls of rice for bait. In the clear sunlit water we could see our rice balls dangling just before the fishes' noses. But apparently they did not find the bait tempting enough, for they looked at it indifferently, then continued haughtily on their way.

We heard Nelson laughing behind us.

'It's no use,' he said, tapping Salmon on the shoulder. 'They'll never catch fish that way.'

'Show us, then,' we pleaded. Nelson only shrugged. 'All right, will you catch some for us yourself?'

Nelson remained adamant. He considered it beneath him to share his secrets with such rank amateurs.

For two days we lazed our way through the reefs, moving in the right direction, but with infuriating slowness. On the third morning we decided to put Nelson to the test.

'Look here – if you're so friendly with the elements why don't you prove it by bringing us a wind?'

'Oh, I shall,' said Nelson, fixing his empty socket upon us.

His method could hardly have been simpler. All that he did was to step to the rail, point his blind eye in the direction from which he wished the wind to come, draw in a great chestful of air and then roar 'Hroosh! Hroosh!'

Aeolus, the wind god, or his south-eastern representative, must have heard Nelson and honoured the request. Very shortly, to our amazement, there were ripples on the water. Before long the sails were filling under a full-bodied breeze. We made Tana Masa by noon, averaging eight knots on the run. Our respect for Nelson and his lore went up considerably.

We sailed straight to the jetty and made fast. A group of curious islanders gathered nearby. Suddenly they all turned and ran from the beach. Presently, from a cautious distance, they seemed to convince themselves that our mission was a peaceful one, for they began moving towards us again. By that time the headman arrived and spoke to them volubly. He broke away and approached us.

'They'll be glad to help you,' he said. 'Just tell them what you need.'

We did, and soon had a supply of rope and sailcloth.

Then Sandy, our other interpreter, who had a pretty good knowledge of the island dialects, reported that he had found a carpenter in possession of some planking who was willing to build us a sleeping-deck in the hold.

The next morning, while we were busy re-rigging the ship, we saw a Malay wearing the white ducks of authority running towards us. When he could get his breath he explained that he was the controller and that he wanted our help.

'What kind of help?' we asked.

'To put down a tribal war,' was the reply.

We could hardly believe our ears, but he explained that the population of the island was divided into two tribes, between whom there was a long-established feud which every now and again broke out into active warfare. The latest conflict was two days old, and without troops or police he found himself powerless to intervene. After our own long series of defeats we were flattered by his request.

The Colonel asked if the natives were armed with rifles. The controller made it plain that the Netherlands Government did not permit natives to have firearms. They were, however, armed with parangs, thin knife-like swords about three feet long.

We held a conference.

'We've got to support the poor chap,' the Colonel said. 'Otherwise he won't have any authority after we leave. Law and order here depend upon his ability to command assistance when he needs it.'

'That's right,' said Limey. 'Just you chaps push off and settle it. Someone's got to stay behind and mind the ship. That's me.'

It didn't take us long to prepare. We donned our khaki drill and buckled on our revolvers.

'Now isn't this something?' observed Crawley, the young curly-haired gunner, as we mustered on the jetty. 'Among the handful of us here we represent six branches of the services – Navy, Artillery, Infantry, Engineers, Signals and Service Corps – all that's missing is the Air Force.'

'Find me the Air Force and I'll take off in one of their crates,' Limey called from the prahu.

The controller led the way to the battlefield. We passed a long, low hut filled with rows of pallets. Moans and cries of pain were coming from it.

'Hey, who's in there?' one of us asked.

'Oh, those are the wounded,' answered the controller, with what seemed to us to be excessive pride.

Crawley went over, put his head in, and came back to report.

'Crikey, the place is full,' he said. 'Some of them have bloody bandages on their heads, and others are cut up pretty badly. I saw one of their parangs. Nasty-looking weapons they are, too.'

We continued, not very enthusiastically, on our way.

'Hey,' Crawley asked the controller, 'how many fighting men are there on each side?'

'About three hundred, I should say.'

'Crumbs!' exclaimed Crawley. 'What if they don't like the idea of our interfering in their war and join forces against us? Six hundred to nine is heavy odds.'

We reached the front. It was only a clearing where one row of Malays with drawn parangs stood glaring unhappily at another row. With a surface briskness and confidence we were far from feeling, we marched down between the two rows of warriors, looking first to the right, then to the left, and staring them insolently in the eye, while keeping our hands on our weapons.

We could think of nothing better to do than to stand there looking fierce and warlike. To our surprise and relief, we soon saw the Malays begin by twos and threes to slip out of line and melt away into the jungle. We held our position until the last warrior had vanished.

The Colonel then suggested to the controller that if he could obtain the consent of the warring chiefs we would undertake to mediate their dispute. The delighted controller led us at once to the compound of one of the warring factions, which was a hollow square of huts. Opposite the main gate was a large council chamber of impressive splendour. Built on heavy piles, it towered to a height of one hundred and fifty feet. The peak of its atap palm roof narrowed to an elegant point made of finely carved wood. In front of the hall were several stone chairs, set up as though for a council meeting, and two stone altars. A footprint was carved on top of one of the altars suggesting an ancient Hindu origin.

The council hall itself was arranged like the interior of a medieval castle, with the common room at one end and a raised platform at the other. We were welcomed by the chief, a grand-looking, tall old man whose ears had been pierced and the holes enlarged to hold a small coin. When we were all seated in a semi-circle he clapped his hands and ordered that green coconuts be brought for our refreshment. In our turn we passed round cigarettes. The palaver was ready to begin.

The Colonel discoursed at great length and with impressive eloquence, while Salmon interpreted, on the evils of war and on the desire of all people to live in harmony with one another. He appealed to the chief as a follower of Muhammad. Allah, he said, wanted peace for his children; and, as his children, it was up to the chief's tribe to see that peace was maintained.

At every pause the chief nodded his grizzled head sagely in profound agreement. When the Colonel had finished, he began to speak: 'Oh yes, I am of the opinion, too, that war is a very bad thing. I do not want war. My tribe does not want war. But,' he added, unconsciously echoing the shibboleth common to all mankind, 'how can we live at peace with our neighbours when they want war and are always making war?' He shook his head; the decorations flashed in his ear-lobes. A look of perplexity wrinkled his wise face.

'It is all very difficult,' he sighed. 'It is all very difficult.'

The Colonel conceded that indeed it was – then promptly presented our offer to mediate with the rival tribe. The chief readily accepted. At once we set out for the other compound, followed by his chattering entourage. We found that this compound was in striking contrast to the other. The council hall was a ruin, the huts dilapidated. There was refuse in the streets and a general air of lassitude prevailed. We also noted a marked difference between the two chiefs. Whereas the first had been vigorous, authoritative and dignified, this one was ancient, slovenly and wily.

The peace conference ritual began, and once again coconuts and cigarettes were exchanged. The Colonel, having had the benefit of a rehearsal, was at the top of his form. His eloquent arguments seemed irrefutable to us. But evidently not so to the rival chief. He listened impassively until the Colonel had finished, and then stated his case.

'But, of course,' he began, 'non-aggression has always been my unfailing policy. I am a man of the highest principles and I have always stood by them. We have been forced to defend ourselves against the aggressive acts of the other tribe. They are so wicked that there is nothing left for us but to show them the error of their ways by our superior strength.'

He looked at the Colonel shrewdly.

'Why is it that you white men take such an interest in our war? You have a war of your own that has been going on for some time, have you not?'

The Colonel admitted that this was so.

'Our war, you know,' the chief continued, 'has been going on for forty years. And since it is of such long and respectable duration, can you tell me why anyone should try to stop it now?'

'How did it begin?' the Colonel asked.

'A young man from that other tribe insulted one of our young women!'

The memory of that indignity seemed to rekindle his rage. His eyes flashed with anger. But the Colonel, undeterred, reasoned with him. Ultimately, the chief calmed down enough to agree to keep the peace – for the time being, at any rate. But he would not shake hands with his enemy. Not even a present of twenty cigarettes could sway him. However, even if we had only brought about a temporary cessation of hostilities we left feeling that we had done something to save face for the controller.

We returned to the prahu, and were just about to weigh anchor when we spotted two natives paddling towards us at top speed. Speaking rapidly and gesticulating excitedly, they told us that they had sighted a Japanese gunboat steaming up between the islands in our direction. They assured us that we need not worry, however. They would pilot us to a creek surrounded by trees where the enemy would never see us.

This was all very well, except that there was not a whiff of wind – only dead flat calm. Fortunately we had six long oars. We manned them at once and pulled like galley-slaves. The *Setia Berganti* was an inert weight. The sun blazed down on the lagoon; sweat poured from us in gallons; our lungs laboured. But the prahu began to move. Fathom by fathom, cable by cable, we moved her over the three miles until we were hidden behind the palm trees. From our safe haven we peered out and watched the Japanese vessel pass us, unaware of our presence. We were happy to see that she was on a course opposite to our own.

Two hours later the 'all clear' was given. Once more we manned the oars. But a breeze had arisen, the sails filled, and we pointed the bow towards open waters. When we came abeam of our former berth the headman from Pini joined us in his outrigger and sailed with us for about an hour. Then, having taken Nelson on board, he came alongside to shake our hands and wish us a safe journey. With a final wave and a cry of 'Salamat jalan', he set his course for the east, while we sailed westward. We felt a deep sense of loss as we watched his outrigger point towards the distant islands. Although we had few things in common, he had been a true friend.

Our island interlude was over. As we watched the last sight of land disappear, we spoke no more of our dreams of a life of ease in a tropical paradise. We were all anxious again to get on with it – to make our way to Ceylon and freedom. Our mainsail was sound; we had a spare one; there was plenty of coconut, and some fresh fruit, in the hold. In fact, we and the *Setia Berganti* were in better shape than we had been for a very long while.

Rather thankfully, we resumed the regularity of shipboard routine, passing the days standing our watches, mending sail and tidying ship. Our mess was not bad. We began the day with a hot breakfast of boiled rice; followed it with a cold luncheon of left-over rice with fruit or coconut; and ended it with a hot dinner again of rice and tinned beef. When we had been in action, biscuits and corned beef were our regular ration and one I thought I'd never want to see again. But now it tasted superb, perhaps because the sea air gave me such a keen appetite. The only sad part was that the beef was in short supply. It would not last many more days.

To our dismay, we found that our water, too, was getting low. The burning heat, the unremitting glare of the sun on the sea, and the salt air drove us nearly mad with thirst. Often in my dreams I imagined myself kneeling down on the moors at home to drink from some ice-cold Highland spring. The water on the ship was unpleasantly flavoured by the oil or petrol from the tins and barrels in which it was stored. I had not known that good fresh water has a taste – a taste of clean sweetness.

Ours was diminishing faster than we were drinking it. This meant that we were sustaining losses at a dangerous rate through evaporation and leakages. We rationed ourselves to a pint a day apiece, thereby hoping the water would last either until we reached our destination or were picked up.

But once we got through the day we could enjoy the better side of life. Each evening after sundown we gathered on the deck for a pleasant social hour. I can see it yet – the sun gilding the sky with its afterglow; the slow, soothing, gentle swelling of the sea as we sat together and joked and smoked and talked. Often these conversations centred on our post-war plans.

One evening the sun had just made its dignified bow over the horizon, leaving us to the half-light and half-shadow that marks the interval between day and night on shipboard. The *Setia Berganti* glided along effortlessly on the ever-rising, ever-falling bosom of the ocean. It was a time of leisure and peace. Anzac lolled beside the tiller. Limey, having finished his galley chores, joined us where we sat cross-legged on the afterdeck or lounged against the roof-top of the hold.

'A glorious great foaming gallon of iced beer's all I need now,' said Limey as he squatted down beside me. 'Otherwise we've just about everything.' Then, anticipating a protest, he added quickly, 'Oh, I know what you're thinking – no women. For the younger chaps, that is – for Crawley here – and Rosie.'

Since Limey talked more than any of us of the women who would be waiting for him in Colombo, we all grinned. His banter expressed what we were all feeling; life at this moment was good.

The Colonel was sitting with his elbows on his knees and his chin in his hands. His pipe, dangling from his mouth, swung gently to and fro with the prahu.

'It's all rather pleasant, I must admit,' he said. 'Might be fun to repeat the cruise after the war. How about you, Limey? What'll you be doing then?'

Limey replied without hesitation. He had made his plans.

'Oh, I'll be in the city during the day, making me packet. Then at night you'll find me in the local, knocking it back with the old soaks. After that I'll make it home to the wife and kids – all in due time – if I have any by then.'

With a definite shake of his head, he concluded, 'No, I won't be doing any cruising. Not in these waters, anyway.'

'Skipper, what about you?'

'Afraid you'll have to count me out, too. I've got responsibilities. It's back to Singapore for me as fast as I can make it, once I've stopped by to pick up my family in South Africa. That's where I sent them when I was mobilized.'

'And you, Rosie?'

'You can count me in,' I said. 'I'll probably be wandering around, anyway.'

'Haven't you any definite plans?' the skipper enquired in surprise.

'Nearest I have to a plan is the Army,' I said. 'Just before the Japs started their attack I was nominated for an appointment to Staff College at Quetta in India. Maybe I'll be able to start with the next course. If I do I'll stay on in the Army.'

'You could do worse,' said the Colonel.

'Isn't there anything else you'd like to do?' the skipper asked.

I thought a moment.

'There is one other thing. After the occupation things are going to be in a mess around here. The Japs will have to get out of Java and Sumatra. We'll have to give Malaya and India more independence. This'll mean that the local nabobs will be looking around for military and political advisers. I might arrange to be around when the booking begins.'

'What? Not planning to become another Raffles, are you?' Anzac raised his eyebrows.

'If I should happen to follow in the footsteps of chaps like Raffles why should I mind?' I said. 'Especially if I could make a fortune doing it. I wouldn't mind having a bash at working behind the scenes, sort of, in power politics. The best place in that game is in the back room.'

'Sounds to me as if you've got it all worked out,' remarked Anzac mildly, looking up from his compass.

'Not the details. They'll come later. But a man has to give a little thought as to where he's most likely to get the butter for his bread, or the caviar to go with his champagne.'

'Now you're talking sense,' Limey chipped in. 'Maybe I'll change my mind and join your cruise after all — *if* you'll provide a ruddy great steam yacht with caviar by the bucket and gallons of champagne. That's *my* idea of cruising.'

'Not mine,' said Anzac. 'I'll be content with a fair day's wages for a fair day's work, three meals a day and a roof over my head.'

'You're crazy!' snorted Limey. 'I'm all for Rosie's idea.

When he gets his job as Adviser-in-Chief to the Sultan of Somewhere, I'm going to join him as Chief Adviser to the Adviser-in-Chief. Between us we'll rake in the dough and live a gloriously sinful life of ease and luxury for the rest of our days.'

Anzac wagged his big head in disapproval and said, 'You two sound like a pair of ruthless rascals to me.'

I had great respect for Anzac as a man, but I thought his views on life were dull and stuffy.

'Not ruthless,' I retorted. 'Realistic. The chaps who do the leading are those who *know* that we live in a tough world and that you've got to be tough to survive.' I turned to Limey. 'Right, Limey?'

'Too right – too right – too bloody right.'

Anzac was unruffled by our loud-mouthed protestations. He replied in his usual calm, detached tone.

'Money and power, and success – they aren't everything, y'know.'

'Oh, aren't they?' I jeered.

'No, they aren't. There's such a thing as decency.'

Limey shrugged. 'Trouble with you, Anzac, is that you're too bloody good for – too bloody good for – too good for your own good.'

He seemed satisfied that he had had the last word. He got up, yawned and went below, leaving Anzac to the tiller, the stars and his thoughts.

Our spirits rose with each passing day. We talked confidently of what we would do when we reached Ceylon. The Japanese and their threat to us were almost forgotten. Every sunrise was bringing us thirty or forty miles closer to our landfall and freedom.

We were beginning to enjoy our life at sea when, without warning, fever struck us. One by one we were confined to our bunks below. It was increasingly harder to make up the complement of a watch. At first we did not know what malady might be loose amongst us. But finally it became clear that only those had it who had gone ashore to sew sail at Pini. Also, the cases began to display common malarial symptoms.

I came on deck every day, took my place at the tiller and scorned the others' misfortunes. Then, when I was on one afternoon watch, I felt strange myself. Everything began to rotate in front of me. I looked at the compass. It rushed backwards and forwards at me. I looked up. Sky and sea cavorted in a mad dance. Nothing was stable, everything was flux and transition. When I felt myself flying through space I knew it was time to give up.

The Colonel saw me slumped by the tiller. He called for help to carry me below deck, where he took my temperature with a whistle of incredulity. It was hot, cramped and dark in the hold. The stenches of former cargoes, of fried fish and coconut, enfolded me in layers of fetid, sticky air. But I was conscious of very little as I lay there on my bunk with a raging temperature.

When at last my fever abated the first thing that impressed itself on my consciousness was not the smells, not the foul air, but the fact that we were moving – moving through the water at a steady speed.

One evening about the middle of April, I was able to make my appearance on deck at the social hour. After my long period of delirium and isolation this was an occasion. My shipmates welcomed me warmly, making me feel good. I thought I noticed a new optimism among them. They laughed easily and spoke more definitely of their plans for the future. I wondered at the change. Presently the skipper said:

'Tell Rosie the good news, Anzac.'

'By my reckoning, Rosie,' said Anzac, 'we're now clear of the danger area. I'd say we're within five hundred miles of our goal. With a bit of luck,' he continued, beaming, 'a Royal Navy patrol may flag us any minute now – and we'll be quids in.'

'Won't we, though,' Limey crowed. 'Quids in and quids out. I'm going to spend all my back pay on a party. And it'll be a whopper. I may even ask you, Rosie.'

'Why wait to celebrate?' said the Colonel. 'Why not have the party now?'

'With what?' Limey wanted to know.

'With a bottle of old Tokay in my kit. This is obviously the moment to use it. Wait, I'll bring it out.'

Murmurs of incredulity followed him below. We wondered how he had come by that bottle in the first place and what had prompted him to take it along in his stripped-down gear, hoarding it for the appropriate moment to celebrate. Limey went to fetch some tin cups. The Colonel returned with a dusty bottle in his hand. Going round the circle, he poured a little wine into each outstretched receptacle.

'Here's to Colombo!' He raised his own cup in a toast.

'On to Colombo!' we all roared in one happy voice.

Limey glanced up at the curving rails, then out at our wake.

'Think of it! At the rate we're going we should hit Ceylon inside of a week!'

We dared think about it now. I visualized Colombo as I had last seen it, when I had gone through there in the early months of 1940 on my way to Malaya. I remembered the thronging docks, the low white buildings along the well-ordered streets under the waving palm trees, the red rickshaws and the white policemen controlling them in their spick-and-span uniforms. I could see Colombo waiting to welcome us. The scene was so real that I could almost reach out and touch it.

The wine tasted refreshingly sweet. By the last light of fading day I could see smiles of relaxation on the faces of my shipmates. The hour ended. We rose, shook the cramps from our legs and went below to give ourselves over to our dreams, leaving only the helmsman at his post.

*   *   *

The following day I had just come on deck to clear my lungs in the fresh morning air when I heard the watch cry out.

'Smoke ho!'

Over on the starboard side I could see a heavy smudge low along the horizon. By this time we were all on deck.

'That's three ships!' the skipper shouted.

'Right, I can see the funnels,' I called.

'Shall we signal?' Crawley asked.

'No! No!' said the skipper. 'As far west as we are, they still might be enemy.' He turned to the helmsman. 'Go on the opposite course,' he said hurriedly. 'Even if they are enemy they may think we're only clueless Chinese or Malays off course.'

Then he had another inspiration.

'Sapper!'

'Yes, old boy?'

'Think you can steer for a while?'

'I think so.'

'You're the shorty of the outfit. Get into that coolie coat and that big straw hat and take the tiller. The rest of you get below.'

The Sapper disappeared and came back within moments, wearing his disguise. In the wide conical straw hat and long jacket he looked so authentically Oriental as he took his position by the tiller that we all laughed in spite of our uncomfortable situation.

By now we were gathered in the smelly hold. With beating hearts and constricted stomachs we waited. All we could see through the hatchway was the Sapper's coolie hat against the vast grey expanse of the morning sky.

'What are they? Can you see yet?' the skipper called out.

'Not quite. They're three ships. That's all I can see.'

No one stirred. Only the slap of water could be heard against the sides of the ship. Then came the Sapper's voice: 'They look like tankers . . . Yes, they are tankers. I'm sure they are.'

'Tankers!' We echoed the word in consternation.

'Are they enemy?' called the Colonel.

'Can't tell yet. But they must be. Ours wouldn't be in these waters.'

Our first hope – that they might be British or American warships – faded. Now we clung hard to another – the hope that the ships would pass us by. A hum of conversation arose as we tried to reassure ourselves. What if they were Japanese? Why should they bother with an old prahu and a Malay crew?

'Where are they now?' the skipper asked.

'They're still coming in our direction.'

We held our breath. Then, 'Still coming . . . still coming . . . still coming . . . they're about a mile off . . . they're abeam . . . they're enemy all right, blast it! . . . they're drawing away from us . . . still drawing away . . . still drawing away . . . they're well past us . . .'

'With a bit of luck we may make it yet,' said Crawley.

'We just might,' we all murmured.

'Oh, my God!' the Sapper groaned. 'One of them is turning.'

I peered over the coaming and saw a tanker steaming towards us, her prow throwing up a wave of snarling white water. I could tell from the slack postures of my comrades that their hopes, like my own, had reached their nadir. My stomach felt full of ice – cold, hard, raw.

We had failed.

I saw the flash of the four-inch gun on the tanker's foredeck. I heard the sharp crack of the explosion. Then there was a *whish* overhead. About fifty yards away a column of water spurted on our beam as the shell struck.

It was all up. Hastily, we threw our log-books overside and our lead bullets after them. We readied our packs and wearily mustered on deck. We waited in utter despair and silence.

The tanker which had fired on us hove within hailing distance. The rails were lined with sailors – Japanese sailors.

'What a bloody awful sight!' said Limey.

'They're armed to the teeth,' I said, as my glance strayed upwards. A whole battery of light guns and machine-guns was trained upon us. 'You'd think we were a battleship.'

An officer in white stood on the foredeck, waving and shouting to us to come alongside. The skipper took the tiller. The rest of us trimmed the sail for the last time. Smartly we sailed up to the tanker, luffed, and brought the prahu within reach of the rope ladder that had been lowered in the meantime.

The ship's side towered above us. A multitude of silent enemy faces glared down on us.

'Make sure you take all your kit with you!' the skipper said. It was his last command.

One by one we clambered up the rope ladder. My throat tightened. Sails set, deserted and crewless, the *Setia Berganti* was skimming smoothly out over the ocean and out of our lives.

On deck two sailors grabbed me roughly. They twisted my arms behind my back. We were all searched and passed into the safe keeping of personal guards. Mine was a nervous petty officer, who kept the muzzle of his automatic pistol pressed tightly against the side of my head. He was so close to me that I couldn't see him properly. I was aware only of a blur of white uniform, a brown-yellow face and a ring of steel against my skull.

'This isn't getting us anywhere,' I thought to myself. So I said in my most persuasive voice, 'Look here, chum, relax, will you? If you'll take that thing away from my head we'll both be more comfortable.'

My well-intentioned remark drew only a mutter and a sputter: 'Curraabgeroshksshgrhh!' The automatic was pressed against me all the more tightly. Standing, my head strained as far forward as humanly possible without losing my balance, I could see the skipper being escorted to the bridge. I noticed an officer coming my way.

'Please,' I begged. 'Tell my friend here I'm not going to escape and I won't hurt him.'

The officer understood English. He barked a quick order, and the pistol was withdrawn.

'Thank you,' I said. Taking heart from his gesture, I asked the officer, 'What are you going to do with us?'

He stopped in front of me, placed his hands on his hips and grinned expansively.

'You will all be questioned one at a time,' he said in clipped artificial English, 'and then you will be shot. You are spies!'

'That's cheerful news,' I thought, as I rubbed my aching skull.

The skipper returned, looking glum. He was taken to the opposite side of the deck under guard so that he could not say anything to us. All day long our interrogation continued. In the afternoon my turn came. I was escorted to a large cabin on one of the bridges. Here I stood facing three officers seated behind a table. Spread out upon it were personal possessions – watches, wallets, cigarettes, toilet kits, a camera and pencils. Suddenly my heart flipped. I was looking at my blue leather wallet – the one my father had given me when I left Scotland. I remembered what was in it. Why hadn't I destroyed that chit? Had they read it? Did they already know that I was formally authorized to raise money and collect arms to encourage resistance among the Malays?

Keeping a poker face, I bowed as stiffly and formally as though I were being presented at Buckingham Palace.

The three officers ducked their heads without rising.

'Who are you?'

'Ernest Gordon.'

'What is your rank?'

'Captain.'

'What is your regiment?'

'The 93rd Highlanders.'

I was allowed to give this much information under army regulations. But no more. From now on I would have to play it by ear. I had difficulty in keeping my eyes away from my wallet.

'Why were you on that boat?'

'Because I didn't want to stay in Sumatra.'

'Where were you before Sumatra?'

'Singapore.'

The officer in the middle fixed me with hard eyes. He snapped out. 'Were you spying for the British Navy?'

'No.'

The three officers held a whispered conference. They seemed satisfied with my answers. One of them said, 'Pick out your own possessions.'

It was all too pat. Were they playing cat-and-mouse with me? Could it be that they had already found the chit and were letting me spring my own trap?

Assuming a nonchalance I did not feel, I stepped forward and picked up a pencil and one or two other objects. Then I reached for the wallet. I felt their eyes upon me. At any moment I expected to hear one of them bark, 'Now!' But the silence prevailed. I picked up the wallet. Then, opening it, I pulled out several snapshots of girl friends and flashed them before the officers with a man-of-the-world air. They nodded understandingly.

'God bless the girl friends,' I muttered to myself, and returned the wallet to my pocket. I then picked out my camera, from which the film had been removed, and my shaving kit.

'You may go,' the senior officer said.

I bowed and thankfully withdrew.

Back in my place on deck, I pantomimed to my guard that I had an urgent appointment in the head or *benjo*. He had relaxed a little now, and nodded his permission. I rushed for it like a man caught short. As soon as I entered and closed the door, I extracted the incriminating chit from its hiding-place in the outside pocket of my wallet, and flushed it joyfully out of my life.

The interviews ended. Once more the skipper was escorted to the bridge, while the rest of us waited in uneasy silence. After what seemed hours he returned. But now he looked pleased.

Our personal guards withdrew. Only one was left, standing some distance away, so we could talk more or less freely.

'It's all right, chaps,' the skipper said. 'The Nips have changed their minds. They're not going to shoot us after all. We're to be treated as prisoners of war and taken back to Singapore for further questioning. Those are orders from Tokyo.'

From then on our treatment improved considerably. We were allowed to move about the deck with some freedom and to drink as much fresh water as we pleased. After so many weeks of our unpalatable stores the water tasted wonderful. We drank our fill and lounged against the rail of the middle deck, gazing out across the ocean. It was empty. I recalled my last glimpse of the *Setia Berganti* as it sailed forlornly away from us.

What had been her fate? I wondered. Did she sail on, crewless, until she reached her destination? Would she wash up on the beaches of Ceylon? Would she become another *Marie Celeste*, a mystery of the sea? Or a legendary ship like the *Flying Dutchman*? Would the green coconuts finally sprout so that she became a floating island somewhere in the Indian Ocean?

In spite of the tight moments she had given us, our memories of her were mainly happy ones.

Four days later we dropped anchor off Singapore. The contrast with what we had seen of it about three months ago was awesome. Then it was a city of the damned, with great flames from the burning oil-tanks billowing skyward in an angry red along the shoreline. Now all was hushed and still; it was a city of the dead.

Before the tanker reached Singapore one of the English-speaking officers told us that we would be subjected to further interrogation when we arrived by the Kempei Tai, or military police. The prospect did not exactly raise our spirits. But it was just as well for our peace of mind that we did not know what we learned later — that the Kempei Tai delighted in the most depraved kind of tortures. This was to be affirmed by the prosecution at the War Crimes Trial of 1946 as follows: 'The whole of this case can be epitomized by two words — "unspeakable horror".'

The expected interrogation never took place. In fact we were treated in the most casual way possible, since liaison between the Japanese Navy and Army was practically nonexistent, owing to inter-service rivalry. After being ferried ashore we were simply dumped on a pier and left there. No one was on hand to meet us or to guard us.

We must have presented a forlorn spectacle as we stood there wondering what the next move would be. We were bearded and barefoot and wore the most bizarre assortment of uniforms. Two British naval POWs were working on a dock close by. One of them looked up from his toil and saw us. He called out, 'Cheer up, chums! It could have been worse!'

After a while a truck rumbled up, guards jumped out and we were hustled inside. We were on our way to the prison camp of Changi, some twelve miles from the docks.

3

OUR HOSTS

So began my three and a half years as a 'guest' of the Japanese. Changi was only the first of a succession of camps in which we were incarcerated, first in Malaya, then in Upper Thailand. Although Changi appeared bleak enough when we first encountered it, that camp seemed a paradise in comparison with those we were to know later.

During the four years of their ascendency the Japanese military violated every civilized code. They murdered prisoners overtly by bayoneting, shooting, drowning, beating or decapitation; they murdered them covertly by working them beyond the limit of human endurance, starving them, torturing them and denying them medical care.

They also had special refinements for those prisoners who did not comply with certain orders. Some were tortured by having their hands crushed in vices; some were filled up with water and then jumped on; some were suspended from a tree by their thumbs; some were buried alive in the ground. The statistics tell their own grim story; four per cent of prisoners held by the Germans and Italians died, as compared with twenty-seven per cent of those in the hands of the Japanese. In the prison camps along the River Kwai the percentage was much higher than this.

It is difficult to keep these atrocities in perspective. They were the result of behaviour codes fostered by the military for their own ends, codes such as Hakko Ichiu, Kodo and

Bushido. These codes also held that the Emperor was divine, that Japan was a divine country and that both had a divine mission to rule the world. Therefore there could be no compromise; it was victory or death, and any cruelty could be condoned.

While the military were in the saddle, this vicious doctrine was unquestioningly accepted and even eagerly carried out. Once the situation changed, an organized attempt was made to expunge these acts of barbarism from the records, as indicated by two orders sent to all prison-camp commandants on 20 August 1945. The first was to the effect that all documentary evidence must be destroyed; the second commanded that all personnel known to have been responsible for atrocities must flee at the earliest possible moment and attempt to conceal all trace of their identities.

Many of the tormentors among the Japanese military delighted in carrying out the cruel mandate of their perverted codes. It is also plain that millions in the Western world still see no connection between their own consciences and mass slaughter and refuse to accept any responsibility for these manifestations.

In rebuttal, the Japanese can point to the thousands of innocent non-combatants killed or horribly burned and maimed by the dropping of the atomic bomb on Hiroshima and Nagasaki.

Both sides undoubtedly justified their cruelties as serving to shorten the war and improve their chances of winning it, as well as saving the lives of their own kind. The result in each case was the same. In the case of the Japanese, the effect on the perpetrators was to render them callous to man's individual inhumanity to man. In the case of the West, the effect on the perpetrators was also that of initiating an ignoble callousness to human suffering.

Changi was a huge camp located on the site of the former

British barracks at the east side of Singapore Island. The buildings still stood but they could accommodate no more than a thousand men. It was surrounded by a barbed-wire fence twelve feet high. Within the fence over forty thousand prisoners lived, cut off from one another in separate compounds.

By the time we arrived the camp was already a going concern. It had been in business for about three months, the time we were occupied in our frustrated voyage of escape. The Japanese had left it to their captives to organize and administer the camp. Officers were not allowed to show any insignia of rank, but they were permitted to command their own units. In this way the normal hierarchy of military life still prevailed and prevented Changi from degenerating into the chaos of anarchy.

The resourceful prisoners had already done much to make their situation bearable. They had built shacks from discarded lumber and fitted them with bunks. They had made bedding of sorts out of old rice-sacks, eating and drinking utensils from soup-tins, and kettles for cooking out of old oil-drums. Luckily we needed little clothing, for the temperatures were consistently high.

I was pleased to find the survivors of my battalion camped in one corner of the prison area. An old friend, Jack Hyslop, invited me to share his shack. The Argylls were better off than most, benefiting from the talents of a gifted rations sergeant, Percy Evans, an old hand at conjuring necessities out of thin air. As I had arrived at Changi bare foot, he promptly came to my aid with a pair of socks and boots.

I adapted quickly to the new life. Morale in the camp was low, especially among the officers, for a variety of reasons. The pain of defeat was keenly felt. Many believed that capture had been too readily accepted. The story going round at the time of surrender had it that the General had given his word to

Lieutenant-General Yamashita that the garrison would be handed over intact. I heard from several sources later that it had been considered bad form to attempt an escape. Later on the Japanese insisted that everyone sign a no-escape pledge. When the prisoners did not comply with this order immediately they were marched to one tiny corner of Changi and kept on a starvation diet until the order was obeyed.

Furthermore, most of the troops had just arrived in Singapore in time to be captured and were so overwhelmed by atrocity stories that they lived in fear and trembling. Such stories were not without foundation. Many of our troops left behind in the jungle had been tortured, bayoneted or shot upon capture. On Black Friday the Japanese had gone through Alexandra Hospital in Singapore, killing by bayonet all patients, doctors and nurses. They had tied hundreds of Chinese hand to hand and massacred them on the beaches or taken them out in barges to be drowned. There was nothing accidental about such massacres; they were carried out according to a well-established pattern. By these actions the Japanese made it clear that they had no intention of abiding by either The Hague or the Geneva Conventions governing the treatment of prisoners of war.

Another factor that contributed to low morale was the insufficiency of our diet. The basic ration was rice amounting to less than twelve ounces per man per day. Meat, flour, sugar and salt were provided in such small amounts that they were hardly worth mentioning. The rice was highly polished and therefore contained none of the essential vitamins, proteins or minerals. The immediate results of this starvation diet were hunger, general depression and 'blackouts'. Next came the host of diseases caused by vitamin deficiency – such as beriberi and pellagra.

Still another factor was the prevalence of 'bore-hole' rumours, so named because it was at the latrines that they were passed on. The rumours were excessively optimistic. For example, although ten of us had just come from Sumatra where we saw the Japanese Navy and Air Force in complete control, we were told again and again that the Americans and British had already captured Java and Sumatra, that a counter-attack on Malaya was to be launched within a few days and that we would soon be released.

A fresh crop of such rumours started up daily; no one ever knew who originated them. Perhaps a rumour would be invented by someone who wanted to cheer up a chum. It would then be magnified by someone else for the same purpose. Before long it would gain velocity and spread through the whole camp, returning at last to the originator completely unrecognizable. The net effect, however, of hopes raised only to be dashed down was disastrous.

If spirits were low, life was not hard physically at this period. We either did chores around the camp, mostly of a housekeeping nature, or we were taken off in work parties to the city to clean up the debris of war or to sweat on the docks, loading loot into Japanese ships. Competition for these jobs was keen, because they made it possible for prisoners to slip into the shops and buy food.

I had not been long in Changi when I was assigned to supervise such a party, loading captured ordnance bound for Tokyo. An officer from another unit whom I knew only slightly came to ask a favour of me. A friend of his was dying of beriberi. He thought that if I could bring him a jar of Marmite – a yeast compound rich in vitamin B – it might save the man's life. I wrote 'Marmite' at the top of my shopping list.

It was my first time on such a work party, but the men knew the ropes well. While half of them pretended to load the ship, the other half systematically plundered the dockside warehouses. They had no difficulty in diverting the attention of the Japanese guards with horseplay, incidents staged for the purpose, or bold-faced bribery.

We were well along in loading a ship when one of the men in the looting details touched my elbow.

'There's a case of Marmite back in the warehouse,' he whispered. 'But if you want some you'd better hurry. They're already at it like a pack of rats.'

I followed him down and through the echoing interior of the warehouse between canyons of packing-cases. We came upon a group of POWs who had just breached a case and were busy grabbing the contents. I pushed in among them just in time to snatch the last jar for my friend. Tucking it quickly under my shirt, I went back to my post.

This was the first time I had ever consciously stolen anything. I realized that a moral problem had been posed. Did the desire to help another to survive take precedence over categorical morality? But at that moment I felt no single pang of remorse.

I found my officer friend pacing up and down, anxiously awaiting me. When I produced the Marmite he insisted on pressing ten Malay dollars into my hand. I had a twinge of conscience. I could justify my theft on the grounds that I had done it to save a man's life. But could I accept money for it?

I hesitated.

'Take it,' he said. 'It's worth much more than that.'

I needed the money. At the moment I had none of my own. This might mean survival to me. I took it and turned away. Our norms were changing.

A few days later I suffered a violent attack of fever. My temperature went up to a hundred and six. Again I was delirious, as on the *Setia Berganti*. I remember only vaguely the British medical officer drenching me with water in a desperate attempt to cool my burning body. My illness was diagnosed as malignant tertian malaria, grave enough to warrant my being admitted to the hospital, which was already overflowing with patients.

Atabrine was not available; there was no quinine; so I literally had to sweat it out. This was but the beginning of a long series of illnesses which were to lead me to the door of death.

When I left the hospital and returned to the Argylls a new problem plagued me: no longer could I stomach the daily ration of rice. Attempts to flavour it with boiled leaves of hibiscus helped little.

One afternoon, while I was grinding rice grains for my cereal next morning, I felt an acute stabbing pain in the abdomen. Examination revealed that in addition to the malaria I was also supporting a colony of intestinal worms. The doctor dealt with them, then broke the news that my appendix appeared twisted and inflamed and would have to come out. Fortunately, there were still some anaesthetics left, although I did not welcome the prospects of an operation under these circumstances. The orderlies stretched me out on a kitchen table, and placed a kerosene storm lantern where it would shed the most light. They laid a pad over my mouth, sprinkled a few drops of ether on it and off I went into dreamland.

Within a day or so I began to feel much better. The operation had been a success. I thought the time had come to speed my recuperation by adding some tinned goods to my diet. For five dollars out of my ten – exactly half my worldly goods – I was able to buy one tin of Campbell's Tomato Soup. I ate it straight from the tin, savouring each mouthful, and rolling it around and around on my tongue before swallowing it. I don't think anything has tasted so delicious since.

When I returned to the Argylls' quarters I was able to make a better appraisal of the prevailing attitudes. One noticeable change from ordinary barrack life was the obvious interest in religion on the part of so many. As disease spread, as spirits became depressed, as hope flourished and died and men had nothing to which they could look forward, they sought aid from beyond themselves.

Church services were allowed by the Japanese. They were held in the open and in general were well attended. Several men whom I knew to have no religious ties went regularly, listened attentively, sang hymns lustily, prayed fervently and read their Bibles. I was not interested in going. It seemed to me that for a good number of them, at least, religion was an attempt to find a quick and easy answer, a release from their fears. In general, although many already Christian undoubtedly benefited from this resurgence of religious feeling, and others received temporary solace from it, it led, in most cases, only to sterility. It appeared to me that, as human resources failed, men turned to God and said, in effect, 'Look here, Old Boy, I'm in trouble. I'll speak well of You if You'll get me out of it.'

So, with many, church-going became a kind of insurance policy to protect them against personal suffering, and religion became a thing of shibboleths, formulas and easy answers. They believed that if they cajoled God properly He could be persuaded to save them from the unpleasantness of their present existence. They prayed for food, for freedom or to be spared from death.

The Bible they viewed as having magical properties; to the man who could find the right key all would be revealed. One group assured me with absolute certainty that they knew that the end of the war was at hand. When I asked them for proof they told me that they had found it in the books of Daniel and Revelation. They went on to demonstrate mathematically how they had arrived at this conclusion. They had manipulated numbers and words from these two books in a way that seemed convincing enough to them.

The men who turned to religion in this and other ways were only putting into practice what they had learned in their impressionable years from their parents and Sunday School teachers, at least of certain persuasions. As children they had doubtless been told: 'If you go to church you are being a good boy and God will reward your goodness by giving you what you want. If you pray for something God is bound to give it to you, provided you pray loud enough and hard enough. If you are in trouble turn to the Bible; there, in the written Word, you will always find the answer.'

The dominant motive for such a wholesale embracing of religion as happened at this time in Changi was not love or faith but fear: fear of the unknown, fear of suffering, fear of the terror that walks by night, fear of death itself. Fear made for division rather than for community.

I had not been long back in camp when word came that the Argylls were to leave for up-country. It was no 'bore-hole' rumour this time; the orders had been seen. The destination was thought to be somewhere in northern Malaya, or possibly Thailand.

I was still weak, but my friends thought that it would be wise if I went along; they surmised that there ought to be a better food supply in the north, and also more chances of making an escape, since it was not so far from Burma. I concurred. Packing was a simple business; I had only to wrap up my blanket, a pair of shorts, two tin cans and a tooth-brush.

Before leaving on our march to the railway station we were gathered together to hear an inspirational lecture by an English-speaking Japanese officer. He began with a long political preamble, reminding us that a new era was coming into being, one reflecting the wisdom and benevolence of the Mighty Emperor of Japan, the greatest ruler ever known. Everyone would benefit from the new justice, so in the place to which we were going we would have nothing to fear. He then went on to extol the glories of the prison camp that had been prepared for us. His phrases sounded like advertising copy for a health resort. Here, he said, we would find not only pleasant quarters and the finest of food, there would be splendid facilities for recreation and the best of care in modern, well-equipped hospitals for those who had the misfortune to fall ill.

We had had enough experience of the promises of our captors not to trust them. At the same time we hoped that we just possibly might find things a little better than we had known. At least we would be in the countryside, where fruit and vegetables ought to be easier to obtain.

We were given two balls of cooked rice apiece, allowed to fill our water-bottles, and then we started for the station, where for the first time in many weeks we were again among other people. Malays and Chinese were waiting in crowds for trains to take them away from Singapore, but we were heavily guarded and forbidden to speak to them.

Finally our train was shunted in and we saw at once that we were not going to travel first-class. We were shoved into small, stifling metal box-cars and the doors were barred after us. There was no room to sit properly, much less lie down. The train moved out of Singapore Island across the Causeway, which the Japanese, in the meantime, had repaired. Through the slits in the cars we could see the bomb craters, the twisted and shattered equipment, the burned-out trucks, all bitter memories to the devastation of war. With a twinge of recollection, the memory of our march on to the island came back to me. It had been only a little over three months before — yet how much had happened in that short time!

As we passed, Malays, Tamils and Chinese stared up at us, sad and sullen. On one of the rare occasions when we were allowed out of the train to relieve ourselves I had the chance to speak to a Tamil who had been a foreman on a rubber estate. I asked him how things were.

'Oh, bad, sir, terribly bad,' he replied, 'and they are getting worse.'

Up into northern Malaya the train moved. At any moment we expected to reach the site of our new camp. But the train kept on going, mile after weary mile, into Thailand. After four days and four nights locked in those cramped, fetid little cars we reached our destination at a place called Banpong.

Our hearts sank as we piled out. We weren't hoping for much, but Banpong failed even our dimmest expectations. It was nothing but a small clearing stocked with bamboo and atap palm. If there were to be any camp at all, it was obvious that we would have to make it for ourselves.

Not one of the promised improvements ever materialized. Nothing was offered in the way of recreation. We slept in huts built by ourselves in long Japanese style on bamboo platforms without bedding of any kind. The only hospital was a hut we so designated. We never saw any of the fresh fruit and vegetables we had envisaged. Latrines were open pits. For bathing we had the river. We hoarded our bits of soap for shaving, and washed ourselves with wood ash from the cook-house fires and dried ourselves with jungle leaves.

Banpong was a long step down from Changi, but worse was to come. Our rations were the same, a small portion of rice of poor quality, in spite of the fact that our regime soon changed to hard labour. We were sent out daily in work parties to hack away at the jungle, clearing ground for other camps such as this one.

As this was a small camp, the Japanese were right on top of us at all times, breathing down our necks. There was no privacy whatever. We were subject to all the diseases of malnutrition. Some men died. There was no chance of escape. We looked out at that thicket of jungle and knew that a thousand miles of it still separated us from the Burma jungle.

We were at the mercy of guards whose ugly native dispositions were not improved by the conditions under which they had to work. It was not uncommon for a guard to work himself up into a maniacal fury over a trifle and strike out at everyone in sight. Once one of the prisoners dared to remonstrate with a guard for what he considered unreasonable behaviour. The guard immediately retaliated by bashing him over the head with the butt of his rifle and then jumping up and down on him until he lost consciousness. Apart from such acts of major brutality the temper of the guards found expression in acts of pettiness. If we passed a guard while walking anywhere we were required to bow low, or be punished. Whatever expression we assumed during roll-call parades we were open to the accusation of looking arrogant, which was regarded as a grave crime against the Emperor, punishable by beating.

These were minor infractions. The major ones were punishable by death. One of these was trying to escape. Another was to be caught listening to the radio. Yet the radio was a life-saver to us. We had smuggled in a tiny set built into the bottom of a water canteen. For this we were indebted to some unknown technicians of the Royal Signal Corps. When Singapore fell they had dismantled their large receiving sets, and from the parts made up a number of little ones. Some of these had found their way into the possession of prisoners at Changi.

With this set we had more news of the progress of the war than at any time before or afterwards. But we were almost daily reminded of the perils of listening to it. At a nearby camp, five men were surprised while listening and promptly kicked to death. This was ordered by a young Japanese officer who spoke English with a marked American accent. He was a graduate of Columbia University.

Most of us were never permitted to know the hiding-place of the set, lest we disclose it under torture. It made its appearance in a new location every night. The most rigorous kind of watch was set by the prisoners to warn against approaching guards. This wireless was to follow us through many camps. Its last hiding-place was in a cook oven. But I never knew where it was concealed at Banpong.

One problem was getting the power with which to operate it. For a time this was supplied by one prisoner who had been pressed into service as truck-driver for the Japanese. Every night when he had finished work he would take the battery out of his truck, hoist it on his shoulder and boldly carry it into camp in full view of everyone.

One night a sentry challenged him as he was passing the guard-house.

'*Bagero!*' the sentry shouted. 'What are you doing with that?'

The truck-driver regarded him with sleepy, innocent eyes.

'Can't you see that it's a very wet night?' he said. 'This battery is very delicate and easily injured by the damp. Therefore I am taking it to my bed to keep it dry.'

The sentry beamed and gave him a packet of cigarettes for his devotion to the Emperor.

However, we could take little cheer from the progress of the war as we learnt it from the radio. Rommel was about to take over in North Africa. The Russians were being pushed back; Moscow itself was in danger. The cities of Great Britain were being pitilessly bombed. The Japanese were still masters in the Pacific.

In spite of these dour tidings, the same old rush of over-optimistic 'bore-hole' rumours started up again. Some of the officers, aware of the devastating effect on morale of the puncturing of these rumours, did their best to counteract their effects. We spent evenings making the rounds of the huts, giving long-range analyses of the war, its cause and consequences as far as we could see them, and the probabilities of the eventual outcome. Whether or not these talks did any good it was difficult to tell.

The officers spared no effort to help bolster sagging morale.

We rooted out all conceivable talent for Saturday-night vaudevilles. I made my contribution by singing some Scottish student songs, 'As Through the Street' and 'A Lum Hat Wantin' a Croon'. I cannot pretend that my efforts were warmly received. This was the first time I had ever sung in public. It was also the last.

All in all, these attempts at diversion and entertainment were something less than successful. Apathy and listlessness settled over Banpong like a miasmic fog. Morale was low and sinking steadily. We were on the long, slow slide – and there was worse to come.

4

THE VALLEY OF DEATH

In September the order came for us to move again. We were to be transferred to another area, somewhere farther north. This time there was no train. We were to march to the next camp, carrying our personal kit, our cooking utensils and our tools, which meant that we were loaded to capacity.

I had not recovered from the effects of my operation; I still had intermittent attacks of malarial fever. Now something new was added to my growing collection of diseases. Shortly before we left I suffered an attack of amoebic dysentery which left me in a constant state of weakness.

In this condition I set out with the others, many of them also feeble with illness, along a jungle road under a scorching sun. I have often thought about that march and the hidden resources of the human mechanism it disclosed. My legs moved of their own accord, as if they had no relation to me, yet I plodded along, almost able to keep up with the column.

As the pitiless sun rose in the sky, its heat intensified our thirst. We walked past endless rice paddies. There, within reach, were lovely enticing pools of muddy water. We had but to lean down, scoop it up with our hands and drink. To do so, however, would be to invite death by cholera or typhoid.

The sun reached its zenith and began to descend. The blaze lessened, but now our bones ached with weariness. In spite of their best efforts, some of the men fell behind.

Twilight came. The guards, who were travelling by truck,

were sent to round up the stragglers. They shouted insults at us which we did not hear and rained blows on us which we could not feel, so great was our exhaustion.

Camp that night was no more than a place to sit on the bare ground. For our supper we were handed a cup of water and a ball of cold rice each. We stretched out where we were and slept.

The guards roused us early for the last lap of our journey, marching us past a village named Kanburi to the bank of a wide, brown, muddy river. The river bustled with activity. Strange native craft, propelled by poles or outboard motors, were busily ferrying supplies from one bank to the other. No one knew the name of the river. We hadn't a clue that this was the River Kwai, and that we were at the very spot where later we would be forced to build a bridge.

Heavy, open wooden barges waited by the river's edge. The guards herded us aboard, until our entire contingent – all two hundred and fifty of us – were jammed into four of them. A ridiculously small motor-launch appeared and began to tow the string of barges. For several hours we stood unprotected in the scorching sun while the spluttering launch pulled its heavy load slowly upstream against the current some two and a half miles to the site of our new camp.

I staggered up the muddy bank from the river and had my first glimpse of Chungkai. Nearby, I saw only loose stacks of cut bamboo, other loose stacks of atap grass and a scraggly, unkempt grass hut, which I took to be the guardhouse. Beyond, wherever I looked, was the jungle – powerful, lush, dark and green, threatening and confining. In front of me was a small clearing.

I sat resting on the ground, trying to acclimatize myself to the jungle environment. We were part of it, hemmed in by the rawness of untamed nature. Above me I could see the fronds of the bamboo forming a lacework pattern against the infinite blue of the sky. A tree rat scampered along a bowing branch, paused, sniffed and scampered again. A tiny delicate bird hovered busily for a while by a trembling leaf, then darted quickly to another tree in its quest for insects. A monkey chattered angrily, scratched itself and swung by, looking for its mate.

I was not allowed to rest for long. The guards came up, shouting, and we were organized into work parties, building our own barracks – the usual scraggly huts of bamboo, roofed with atap palm, with sleeping platforms made of split bamboo rising just above the mud and extending down either side of the long narrow interior. A hut housed about two hundred men, and each man had to himself an area about six feet long and two feet wide – roughly the room of a narrow grave.

We cleared an area of something like three-quarters of a mile long by half a mile wide, pushing back the jungle for a time. Between the huts was earth – trampled earth, the dark-brown colour of mud in the wet season, the light-brown colour of dust when it was dry. In the wet season everything we touched oozed mud. The dust in the dry season caked our skins, stung our eyes and choked our throats.

We had not been long at Chungkai when we found out why we were there and why the camp existed. We learned it piece by piece from what we saw, from 'bore-hole' rumours and from remarks incautiously dropped by the guards. The more we learned, the greater grew our foreboding.

In violation of all international conventions, we prisoners of war were to be used to build a railway for the Japanese Army. Field Marshal Juichi Terauchi, of the Japanese southern army, had formally filed the request for our services and Tojo himself had approved it. The enemy was planning to go on through Burma and ultimately to invade India. Since their existing supply line was by sea, and therefore vulnerable to submarine attack, they planned a substitute route overland. The Japanese wanted to take advantage of two rail-lines already in operation – one running from Singapore to Bangkok and one in Burma between Rangoon and Ye. All that was needed to join the two lines was a railway to be cut through hills and jungle running from Banpong up along the River Kwai and thence through the Three Pagodas Pass to connect with the Burma line north of Ye on the way to Moulmein.

This railway was to be several hundred miles in length through difficult terrain. When the Japanese engineers made their first calculations they estimated that it would take five or six years to complete it. Once they received the go-ahead to use prisoners as labour they cut the projected time to eighteen months.

The building of the railway was scheduled to begin in June 1942. But for reasons which we never knew construction did not get under way until almost November. In spite of this late start, the target date for completion, to fit in with the Japanese invasion time-table, remained the same – October 1943. An undertaking that appeared impossible to bring off in eighteen months thus had to be compressed into twelve. To hide their nervous tension, the Japanese took to bawling and shouting, which only compounded confusion with confusion. The prisoners bore the brunt of their wrathful frenzy.

To get the job done, the Japanese had mainly human flesh for tools, but flesh was cheap. Later there was an even more plentiful supply of native flesh – Burmese, Thais, Malays, Chinese, Tamils and Javanese – more than sixty thousand of them, all beaten, starved, overworked, and, when broken, thrown carelessly on that human rubbish-heap, the Railway of Death. But in the earlier stages of the construction the Japanese used chiefly the helpless bodies of their prisoners of war.

Thus began the most gruelling phase of our ordeal. Every morning, as soon as dawn streaked the sky – at about 5.30 or 6 o'clock – we were marched out of Chungkai to work at hacking out the right of way for the railway. We were not marched back until late at night. Sometimes, if there was a job to be finished, we were kept at work into the early hours of the next morning. As officers, we did not actually work with pick and shovel, but had consented to supervise our men while at work. We kept the same hours as they did.

This was our routine seven days a week. There was no day of rest, no holiday, no hiatus of any kind. We lost all consciousness of time. There were so few meaningful incidents to serve as markers. Was it Tuesday the fourth or Friday the seventeenth? Who could say? And who would care? One grey day succeeded another – with no colour, no variety, no humanity. Misery, despair and death were our constant companions.

Our first tasks were to hack out the jungle, to swing our picks, to shovel earth into big grass baskets and carry them to fill in a level roadbed. Except for our G-strings, we worked naked and barefoot in heat that reached one hundred and twenty degrees, our bodies stung by insects, our feet cut and bruised by the sharp stones.

The monsoons came early that year and with them a new adversary was added. We worked and lived in a world of wetness. One day's labour would be washed away by the floods of the next. Torrents strewed rocks in our path. We understood then how unfortunate was the location of our camp at the juncture of the Kwai and the Mea Klong. When the rains came both rivers overflowed and left us living on a raft of mud. It spread its clinging ooze throughout the whole camp and came nearly up to the level of our sleeping platforms.

Towards the spring of 1943, the Japanese grew increasingly nervous that the railway wouldn't be finished on time, and vented their anxiety on us. Somewhere the guards had picked up the word, 'Speedo'. They stood over us with their vicious staves of bamboo yelling 'Speedo! Speedo!', until 'Speedo!' rang in our ears and haunted our sleep. We nicknamed the project 'Operation Speedo'.

When we did not move fast enough to suit them – which was most of the time – they beat us mercilessly. Many no longer had the stamina to endure such beatings. They slid to the ground and died.

Our work parties moved on into the hills, where the right of way had to be dug and blasted from solid rock. Here the job was not only harder but a good deal more dangerous. In any undertaking so arduous there were bound to be accidents. But our overseers multiplied them by causing many unnecessary deaths and injuries. Human life was cheap; they simply did not care.

A guard, enraged over some trifle, would shriek a curse, then hurl a hammer at a prisoner's head. A Japanese engineer carefully instructed two prisoners in making ready a dynamite charge. While they were still carrying out his instructions he touched off the charge and blew them to pieces. A boulder was mysteriously pushed off a ledge, crushing a group of workers clearly visible below. The white of the limestone was stained red with prisoners' blood.

Death was everywhere. Men collapsed in their tracks, from thirst, exhaustion, disease and starvation. But Death did not work fast enough for the Japanese, so they tried to assist him in his grim harvesting, as they drove on the work of the railway.

The bridge over the River Kwai, an important link in the rail system, was built in the spring of 1943. Since the Japanese had no steel to spare, and no heavy construction equipment available, the bridge was built by hand labour – our labour. Several hundred yards in length and about five storeys above the water, it was a sizeable engineering job, but one that was primitive by modern standards.

Heavy square beams of timber were floated out into the river by work parties. The beams were then tilted upright and driven into the river-bed by hand-operated pile-drivers. They were then held in place by cross-beams. Other sections, also held together by cross-beams, were erected on top of them until the bridge rose to the level of the track.

Much has been made of the building of this bridge, but it was, in fact, a relatively minor episode in 'Operation Speedo'; there were in fact other bridges of a similar nature. Construction of it was finished in less than two months, whereas it took a year to build the railway. The bridge claimed its toll in lives, but men died in thousands on the railway.

At first the Japanese had respected the international law which stipulated that officers were not to perform manual labour, and were to be employed as supervisors only. But the time very soon came when they ordered us to work with tools. This was a difficult dilemma, for this meant that we were being forced by the Japanese to contravene the international law which forbade the use of officer-prisoners as manual workers. We refused to obey the Japanese command, whereupon we were told that unless we worked we would get no food at all. Still we refused.

'Very well, we'll kill you if you don't,' said the Japanese.

We replied, 'All right, go ahead.'

Then we waited for our answer. It was not long in coming. All ranks were ordered on parade. Officers were lined up on one side – the other ranks across from them. The guards 'rammed one up the spout' and trained the sights on our Jocks.

'Now will you work?' the Japanese asked us once again. This time we could only answer 'Yes'. And so it was that British officers joined their men, as coolie labour, in building the bridge over the River Kwai.

One interpretation of this situation – namely, that British officers built this bridge in record time to demonstrate their superior efficiency – has been widely publicized through Pierre Boulle's novel *The Bridge on the River Kwai*, and the film based on it. The story was an entertaining fiction, but to let such an impression go unchallenged in any factual account would do an injustice to the officers and men – living and dead – who worked on that bridge. They did not do so willingly, but at bayonet point and under the bamboo rod, and they risked their lives continually seeking for an opportunity to sabotage the bridge.

These jobs were done by men who worked out from Chungkai and such camps in the vicinity. Chungkai itself was the base for similar camps strung out eastward along the river and the railway for several hundred miles to the Three Pagodas Pass over near the Burmese border. To begin with, Chungkai was a busy staging area, a mustering point of materials and fresh men; in the end it became a fetid hospital camp where the broken returned to die.

The sleazy huts grew to number forty. At the peak they housed nearly eight thousand, a battered population, but one that was ever changing, ever shifting. Batches of new POWs arriving from Malaya replaced old hands as they were marched off to other camps farther up country. Friends, old comrades-in-arms, came and went, appeared briefly and disappeared. A few we saw again months later; many we saw no more. A thousand men left us to work on some unnamed project and were never heard from. Smaller groups vanished often without trace. Now and then I recognized in a batch of new arrivals the face of a former barrack-mate. He would be gone before I could greet him. We lived in a constant state of flux, never knowing what the next day held for us.

In Chungkai we were being slowly starved. We were doing heavy work now, but our rations were no more than when we had been on light work. There were meagre quantities of meat, oil, tea and sugar, very occasional vegetables, and sometimes salt, but these were in such tiny quantities that they were of hardly any nutritional value. Our diet was rice, three times a day; and it was rice of the poorest quality, the sweepings from the godowns. Much as we hated it, rice might have kept us going had there been enough of it. But the most officially allotted to each man was four hundred and twenty grams a day. This figure was purely hypothetical, for so many Japanese quartermasters dipped into the supply along the line that far less than that was left by the time the rice reached us.

Rations were issued on the basis of heads counted for work; no rice whatever was allotted for the sick. It seemed to be the fixed policy of the Japanese High Command to write off the sick as quickly as possible and to waste no food on them while doing it. After a few months even these scanty rations were further reduced to provide, so we were told, better sustenance for the workers back home in Japan. It can be imagined how happy this news made us.

Starvation and the lack of proteins and vitamins in our daily diet gave the diseases of malnutrition a chance to get in their deadly work. More and more men went sick every day.

We thought much of escape, but escape was next to impossible. It was fairly easy to break through the flimsy twelve-foot bamboo fence. Although guards were stationed at several points around the perimeter of the camp, and others patrolled at regular intervals, they could be eluded. But if a man broke through, where could he go?

A thousand miles of jungle was the stoutest fence that could surround any camp. To be caught outside the camp meant death – immediate death at the hands of violent guards or slow death by starvation. We were not deterred by the wild animals or by the multitude of poisonous snakes in which the jungle abounded. It was the jungle itself, impersonal, menacing, trackless, that shut us in. More actively hostile were the natives, for the POW had a price on his head and the Japanese had set the price high. Of those who attempted to escape there is no record of any surviving.

Four of our number proved how slight the chances were. They slipped through the bamboo enclosure only to be reported by natives, captured and brought back. We next saw them pegged out on the ground in front of the guardhouse. The Japanese made a point of letting us all know that they had been tried and sentenced. Next morning at dawn we reported as usual for work parade, knowing full well what was to happen at that moment. A ragged volley of rifle-fire rang out; a short silence followed; then, one by one, four single shots from a pistol.

Our friends had made good their escape – in the only way possible from Chungkai.

The same fate might have been mine. Jack Hyslop and I had long plotted an escape. But when the hour came I went down with one of my recurrent attacks of malaria and could not join him. Jack went anyway. But his native contacts whom he was to meet outside failed to appear as they had agreed to, and Jack was fortunately able to get back inside the fence before he was missed.

The only purpose in breaking through the fence, therefore, was to trade on the black market with the local Thais or to forage for fruits and plants that could be used as substitutes for medicines. The villages were tiny, collections of no more than six or seven huts scattered along the Kwai not far from the camp. Here the Thais cultivated their rice paddies or fished in the river. Their existence was frugal and they had little to spare.

Many of the prisoners still had an occasional penknife, fountain pen or a remnant of clothing such as a pair of shorts or a shirt. These were prized by the Thais and brought high prices. From time to time enterprising traders turned up, travelling by river. Then wares were available at a price, including tinned milk and tobacco.

Lime trees, some banana trees and red chillis grew in a semi-wild state at the edge of the villages. We also bartered for these, or, when the occasion permitted, helped ourselves. Such expeditions were always dangerous.

Death called to us from every direction. It was in the air we breathed, the food we ate, the things we talked about. The rhythm of death obsessed us with its beat – a beat so regular, so pervasive, so inescapable that it made Chungkai a place of shadows in the dark valley.

It was so easy to die. Those who decided that they had no further reason for living pulled down the shades and quietly expired. I knew one man who had amoebic dysentery. Compared with the rest of us he was in pretty good condition. But he convinced himself that he could not possibly survive, and he did not. An Allied naval lieutenant reached the point where he could no longer endure his misery and tried to commit suicide. He did not succeed in his attempt, but died shortly afterwards with nothing wrong with him; he died from failure of the will to live.

These were the day-to-day cases of death retail. At times we were also brought face to face with death wholesale. On one occasion a whole string of barges came floating down-river to our camp. They were the barges of the dead. Their cargo consisted of corpses – the bodies of men from up-country who had been starved, overworked, corrupted with disease – no more than skeletons covered with skin. When the Japanese could use them no longer they loaded the bodies on barges. Why, no one knew. Perhaps they planned to reload the barges with living POWs and send them upstream as replacements.

Without warning, cholera struck. All around us, on the job, in the hut, men suddenly became violently sick. They were carried away to the isolation area. We knew that we would never see them again. Cholera victims were not buried as were those who died daily; they were burned. Details were assigned to drag the bodies to the river-bank. On great blazing pyres were placed the remains of men who had once been husbands, sons, lovers, friends. While the flames crackled around them in the shimmering heat, they would turn, kick, bend and reach, then rise in a macabre dance – their eerie dance of farewell.

As conditions steadily worsened, as starvation, exhaustion and disease took an ever-increasing toll, the atmosphere in which we lived became poisoned by selfishness, hate and fear. We were slipping rapidly down the slope of degradation.

In Changi the patterns of army life had sustained us. We had huddled together because of our fears, believing that there was safety in numbers. We had still shown some consideration for each other. Now that was all swept away. Existence had become so miserable, the odds so heavy against survival, that, to most of the prisoners, nothing mattered except to survive. We lived by the law of the jungle, 'red in tooth and claw' – the law of the survival of the fittest. It was a case of 'I look out for myself and to hell with everyone else'.

This attitude became our norm. We called it 'The Ladder Club'. Its motto was 'I've got the ladder up, Jack. I'm all right'. The weak were trampled underfoot, the sick ignored or resented, the dead forgotten. When a man lay dying we had no word of comfort for him. When he cried we averted our heads. Men cursed the Japanese, their neighbours, God. Cursing became such an obsession that they constructed whole sentences in which every word was a curse.

Everyone was his own keeper. It was free enterprise at its worst, with all the restraints of morality gone. Our captors had promised to reduce us to a level 'lower than that of any coolie in Asia'. They were succeeding only too well.

Although we lived by the law of the jungle, the strongest among us still died, and the most selfish, the most self-sufficient, the wiliest and shrewdest, perished with the weak, the generous and the decent. Dostoevski described a condition like ours when he said in *The Brothers Karamazov*:

> For he is accustomed to rely on himself alone and to cut himself off from the whole; he has trained himself not to believe in the help of others, in men and humanity, and only troubles for fear he should lose his money and the privileges he has won for himself.

This pervasive selfishness was not universal. As I had occasion to learn myself in a practical way, there were several men who, in the midst of the widespread degradation and despair, kept their integrity inviolate and their faith whole. The officers, as much as the other ranks, however, became subject to the same decay of morale. In the early stages of Chungkai, when they supervised the men instead of working beside them, as later, a number of them had that eroding leisure that, in such conditions, leads men to brood on their own miseries; others, too, with the props of the military structure removed, became cynical, bewildered or despairing.

For most of us, little acts of meanness, suspicion and favouritism permeated our daily lives. Even the drawing of our meagre ration was a humiliating experience. To get our meals, we formed a line in our huts. Our server would dip his can into the rice bucket and dump its contents into our mess-tins. Another server would ladle out a watery mess of green leaves.

I always watched warily when my turn came. I knew that the servers would give me short measure so that they would have more for themselves and their chums. Yet I dared not protest, lest I should draw even shorter measure at the next meal-time. I knew this – and I knew that they knew that I knew. I hated them for knowing. And I hated myself for hating them.

There were depths below depths to which some, discarding

the last pretence of self-respect, yet descended. The minute roll-call was over in the evening there would be a rush to the Japanese cookhouse. The cooks would bring out swill-pails and set them on the ground. Standing back, they folded their arms and looked on with self-satisfied smiles while prisoners pushed, kicked and shoved one another out of the way as they fought for scraps from the enemy table.

One evening this too-familiar scene was taking place as I passed by. A wretch broke away from the pack and stumbled towards me. In his hand he clutched a soggy mess of rice and stew. Drops of gravy dripped through his fingers. He had turned his back on the others, lest they should see what he had and be tempted to rob him. A wolfish leer contorted his face as he craftily licked at his spoils.

'Rather than do that,' I thought to myself, 'I'd die!'

He passed me at a kind of trot, like an animal going to his lair, except that an animal would have had more dignity.

It was common practice for prisoners to steal from one another. A Malayan rubber planter named Iain Stewart, whom I had known in Singapore, turned up in Chungkai. He was pleased to find someone he knew. The next day when I saw him again he was disconsolate.

'What's wrong, Iain?' I asked.

He could hardly speak.

'My pack's been taken,' he said at last. 'Some lousy bastard snatched it right from under my head last night. I've lost every bloody thing that I had in the world – my fiancée's photograph, my knife, pen, notebook – the things I've hung on to all the way. But what hurts worst is to be robbed by your own kind.'

'Did you shout?'

'Yes I shouted. But no one lifted a finger to help me. I ran after him, but he got away in the confusion. By God, I never thought I'd see the day when a thing like this could happen.'

Overcome with emotion, he removed his steel-rimmed glasses and wiped them on the strip of canvas that served to cover his loins.

'At least you have those,' I said, trying to cheer him up.

'Yes, I'd be as blind as a bat without them and that would have been blinking awful, wouldn't it? I stuck them in a piece of bamboo at the foot of my sleeping platform so I wouldn't roll on them. It was lucky I did.'

'Have you reported this?'

'Oh yes. I went straight off to see the British colonel. Nothing can be done about it. Goes on all the time. We can't control it among ourselves, and the Nips don't give a damn. In fact, the more depraved we become, the more it pleases them.'

'How they must be gloating over us! The white man and his civilization! What a pompous fraud!'

'Damnable, isn't it?' said Iain, as he adjusted his glasses.

Even more damnable than those who stole from the living were the human jackals who lurked about waiting to rob the dead. Most of the prisoners left this world picked as clean as Iain. The jackals were not above snatching their last few rags. What added spice to their nefarious game was the hope that they might find a watch, a ring, a knife, a pen or even a pound note stitched into a loincloth that had been overlooked. Such items were invaluable, for they could be sold to the Japanese guards or bartered to Thais in the villages for food, canned milk, cigarettes and, on rare occasions, medicines.

This ghoulish activity characterized our general attitude towards the dead. We could see only one end for us all and that was death. Death pressed in all around us; it was never far from our thoughts.

We had no church, no chaplain, no services. If there were men who kept faith alive in their hearts they gave no visible sign. At Changi many had turned to religion for the first time. But the crutch had not supported them; so they had thrown it away.

Many had prayed, but only for themselves. Nothing happened. They sought personal miracles – and none had come. They had appealed to God as an expedient. But God had apparently refused to be treated as one.

We had long since resigned ourselves to being derelicts. We were the forsaken men – forsaken by our friends, our families, by our Government. Now even God seemed to have left us.

One hot afternoon, while we were digging to make a flat foundation for the railway bed, our guards moved away for a minute. Our detail had a chance for a brief respite; we stood mopping our foreheads, slapping at insects or leaning on our shovels. Suddenly a work-mate standing next to me said, 'Have you ever thought how deliberately we choose death?' I told him it hadn't occurred to me. 'From quite early in life we rush to throw in our lot with it,' he went on. 'Our education prepares us for it. We're taught that it's manly and heroic to die; the finest thing that can happen to us is to have our names inscribed on a bronze plaque.'

He wiped the sweat from his forehead with his arm.

'Now, women have more sense. They choose life – and they fight like hell for it – for the life they carry in their wombs and the children they have borne. Why can't we see things the way they do?'

He gazed out over the impenetrable green mass that separated us from the lives we had known.

'I had a woman once. She loved me. In fact, she was crazy about me. When I was called up I went round to see her to tell her it was all over, thank you very much. She couldn't believe what I said to her, so I had to tell her all over again: "It's finished, washed up, *kaput*," I said. "There's a war on or going to be very soon and I'm off to it. Love and war don't belong together and I don't want you grieving, so that's that." I'll never forget the pain in her eyes; God, she was lovely – lovelier even than she had been before, now that I was leaving her – with the pain showing in her eyes and all.

'Before I went away she came to say goodbye. She said that she wanted me to have a book and she handed it to me. I looked at the name on it. It was by some Chinese bloke and it was called *The Importance of Living*. Bloody rummy, wasn't it?' He sighed. 'What a fool I was!'

Then he went on to recite something like this — a poem he had made up or memorized:

I looked within your eyes
and saw the pain you felt —
pain that was for me
because I did not understand
why you gave so much
nor why you tried to cross the chasm
that separated me from you.

We had touched, my love,
that we had, flesh to flesh,
but I had never met you
and you were hurt
yet though you were hurt
you waited —
and then I came to tell you
I was going away
with a flip 'goodbye'
not caring, not caring for you
with the pain-struck eyes.

And I went, went to the battle
that called me from you,
called me from love,
called me from happiness,
called me to where the bloody gutters
run with life,

life that once had danced and laughed
and dared to hope —
and there's no return.

When he had finished he fell silent. This was one of those times when silence is the only bond of understanding. I was silent, too. The Japanese guard came back. We picked up our shovels and resumed digging.

For days afterwards I looked for this work-mate – but I never saw him again.

The hospital in this camp was known as the Death House. So far I had been able to keep out of it. Despite my dysentery and bouts of malaria, I kept on my feet. But one day I had a very sore throat. I borrowed a mirror. At the back of my throat was a great yellow-white patch of blood-flecked phlegm. I didn't pay much attention to it; we couldn't concern ourselves with minor ailments.

Every now and then I tried to remove the patch, thinking that would help. Eventually I succeeded and forgot about it. But I awoke one morning to find that I couldn't talk properly. What was more troublesome, I could neither eat nor drink. Every time I tried, the rice or water would come gushing back through my nose.

I reported to one of the medical officers, a doctor from Glasgow. He found my attempts to speak to him more amusing than I did, and he responded by mimicking me.

By that time I had a pretty good idea what was wrong with me. The blood-flecked patch and the fallen palate were both symptoms of diphtheria. I was sure the doctor knew too. But the pressure on him to produce workers must have been too great for him to pay any regard for my plight. So back to work I went. I soon noticed that I was losing sensation in my legs. They felt as heavy as lead; before long I couldn't lift one after the other.

I went back to the MO. This time he diagnosed the trouble as polyneuritis, a consequence of the diphtheria. Work was impossible because I couldn't stand.

'The hospital for you,' said the doctor.

This time I was headed for the Death House. However, I was so ill that I didn't much care. But I was hardly prepared for what I found there. The Death House had been built at one of the lowest points of the camp. The monsoon was on, and, as a result, the floor of the hut was a sea of mud. And there were the smells; the smell of tropical ulcers eating into flesh and bone; the smell of latrines overflowed; the smell of unwashed men, untended men, sick men, of humanity gone sour, of humanity rotting. Worst of all was the sweet, evil smell of bed-bugs by the million, crawling over us to steal the little flesh that still clung to our bones.

Men lay in rows head to feet. Yet one of the worst features in this jam of humanity was the loneliness; one never really knew one's neighbour. Everyone was crowded together, but there was no conversation, no communion, no fellowship.

On my first day there I passed the time watching the man whose head was at my feet. I wondered where he'd come from and what his name was. He lay there, scarcely moving. Suddenly he jerked up into a sitting position, twitched, fell back and lay still. Flies clustered on his nose and mouth. Then I knew that he was dead.

The swarming flies struck me as obscene. I leaned down and tried to wave them away from him. It was no use. I shouted for the orderlies. It was a long time before they came. Poor chaps. The living were their first concern. What could they do in the face of such suffering?

As the days dragged by, I grew more and more frail. I was no longer hungry; I had passed that stage. I did not suffer, for my body was beyond pain. Yet I continued to live.

Since I had no way of looking at myself, I was unaware of the change in me. I was lying there in a half-stupor, watching the pattern the light made through the ragged atap palm, when I saw two familiar figures. One was my old ship-mate, Edward Hooper, who had been skipper of the *Setia Berganti*, the other was Joe Allen of the Argylls. They must have recently arrived at Chungkai and had come to the Death House looking for me. Slowly they moved along between the sleeping platforms. I called out to them. But it was as in one of those dreams in which you shout and shout and cannot make yourself heard. Although I strained my vocal cords, I could barely whisper.

They had reached the end of the hut and had not seen me. They turned and were on their way out. Just in time I caught the attention of an orderly. He ran and stopped them at the door and brought them to my side. They stared at me, but there was no sign of recognition in their eyes. I plucked at Hooper's wrist. He bent over me. When he was close enough to me I muttered my name.

'Good God!' he exclaimed. 'You can't be Rosie!'

I nodded. On the prahu, when he had given me my nickname, I had a good two hundred pounds of energetic flesh on a solid six-foot-two frame. We chatted a while – or, rather, they chatted – and I nodded or shook my head, and then they left. After they had gone I asked for a mirror. I did not recognize myself. Haunting, sunken eyes stared out at me above a beard. Waxy skin stretched over protruding bones. The swelling at my ankles, the oedema caused by beriberi, was the only fleshy part on me.

The last shreds of my numbed sensibilities rebelled against my surroundings – against the bed-bugs, the lice, the stenches, the blood-mucous-excrement-stained sleeping platforms, the dying and the dead bed-mates, the victory of corruption. This was the lowest level of life. The doorway to death was no noble stepping-off place – but a sordid snuffing-out place, a 'not-with-a-bang-but-a-whimper' sort of place.

A couple of nights later I signalled a passing orderly.

'For God's sake, get me out of here!' I begged with as much force as I could muster.

'Can't,' he said with a shrug.

'Why not?'

'No other place to go.'

'Come off it. There must be somewhere.'

'No.'

'How about letting me lie at the entrance? It's cleaner there and I'd get some air.'

'Can't. The MO wouldn't stand for it. You'd be in our way.'

'How about the far end, then?'

'Can't. That's the morgue.'

'What's wrong with the morgue?'

'Nothing. Except that that's where we put the dead bodies.'

'It's cleaner than this, isn't it?'

'Aye.'

'Then move me!'

'Okay, then. If that's how you want it. You won't be in the way there.'

He had an afterthought – a grisly one.

'But mind – if anyone puts a rice-sack on you while you're sleeping make a noise or move or something. We wouldn't want to bury you unintentionally.'

He called down the hut to his mate.

'Hey, Bill! Here's a live one who wants to go to the morgue. Come on – give us a hand.'

Bill came along and between them they dragged me to the far end. There was no sleeping platform there. I had to lie on the ground, but at least the ground was dry.

As I slept that night I dreamed. I was happy with my dreams. Then my waking senses, dragged reluctantly from their drowsing rest, experienced anew the corrupt smells of dying things – of decaying flesh, of rotting men.

The harsh light of dawn filtered through the ragged atap roof.

5

MIRACLE ON THE RIVER KWAI

My good friend Tom Rigden, who had operated the escape service with me on the Indragiri River, had been captured at Padang and had recently been brought to Chungkai to work on the railway. One evening he came to see me in the Death House. He wanted to tell me that he had organized the building of a tiny hut which I was to have all to myself. My fate was a matter of concern only to some of my fellow POWs. The Japanese had already written me off. All that I needed, therefore, was permission from the British medical officer to be moved.

When the MO was making his morning rounds, I whispered to him.

'Doc . . .'

'Yes?'

'How about letting me out of this hole? Some friends of mine have built a little shack for me. There's not much more you can do for me, is there?'

'No, Ernie, there isn't,' he said. 'I only wish there were . . .'

He looked up and down the Death House, then back at me, lying on the ground in the morgue.

'The only reason for keeping you here is to isolate you from some of the healthier lads. A hut of your own would do that as well and be a lot more comfortable for you. Tell you what – I'll ask the senior medical officer when he comes around. Okay?'

'Okay,' I said.

I watched him continue on his rounds, pausing to chat with each of his wretched patients and encourage them all with his gentle smile.

Within an hour he was back with the SMO. They stood beside me while the MO presented my case. The SMO hesitated.

'I could look in on him every day,' said the MO. 'He's a friend of mine, anyway, and I always like to have a word with him. What do you think?'

They moved away a little beyond what they thought was my listening range. But I could still hear them.

'Had a pretty rugged time of it, has he?' said the SMO in a low voice.

'He's had the works,' the MO answered. 'Malaria, dysentery, beriberi, plus some queer kind of blood infection we can't identify. Oh yes, and he's had an appendicectomy. And on top of that a bad case of "dip" which left him without the use of his legs.'

'What's his present condition?'

'His blood count is way down. And his pulse is very weak.'

'Too bad.' The SMO shook his head. 'The only thing left is to let him have a decent end.'

He looked questioningly at the MO.

'How's he going to look after himself? He can't walk, can he?'

'No, he can't. But I'm sure his friends will help him. It won't be for long, in any case.'

The SMO nodded decisively. The MO came back to my side.

'It's all right. You're free to go whenever you can be picked up.'

I thanked him and the two men moved on. The death sentence had just been pronounced on me by two experts. I had faced death before: once in my early pilot-training days when I had crashed in a disabled plane; once when I had looked into the angry eye of a machine-gun sending its bullets thudding into my shoulder; again at the time of our capture when we were all told that we would be treated as spies and shot. There had been other occasions, too, familiar to most men who have been in action. Death, after all, is part and parcel of the soldier's trade.

This time, however, the business of dying seemed so much more matter-of-fact. Here in the prison camp it was 'the done thing'. The only variable, as far as I could see, was the time – when? Then I found myself resisting the whole idea. 'When?' for me was not now. I was not going to die on my back like an old man.

I recalled the long faces and solemn words of the doctors. Going to die, was I? With a grin, I answered myself in the words of Eliza Doolittle, 'Not bloody likely!'

I tried to support my determination with argument.

'Doctors are naturally pessimistic,' I thought; 'they have to be. But they've made mistakes before and they'll make them again. This time I'll be the one to prove them wrong. I am *not* going to die.'

Reason, however, had a voice of its own. It made itself heard now: 'Why should you be so different? I'll bet others before you have said the same thing, and yet they have died. The doctors have seen a lot of men go out. They know what they're about, don't they? What makes you think they're wrong this time? Why not face up to the facts and bow out as gracefully as you can?'

I wasn't giving in. But to please my troublesome friend, Reason, and to quiet his nagging voice, I conceded, 'Okay. In case I should kick the bucket, I'll try to leave my affairs as tidy as possible.'

In my pack, which I used as a pillow, I had a pencil stub and some scraps of paper. Propping myself up on one elbow, I wrote a letter to my parents:

Dear Mum and Dad,

If one of my friends passes this on to you it will mean that I've guessed wrongly and that I'm not coming back. I'm sorry. I'd have made it if I could. When I made the break, first from Singapore and then from Sumatra, I thought I was bound to return to you safely.

Don't have any regrets. I suppose it just couldn't have been otherwise. I've enjoyed life. I'm glad I was brought up in the country with the sea at the front of the house and the hills at the back. I'm glad I had you as parents. If I seldom showed any sign of appreciation for all the love and kindness you've given me, it was because I took it too much for granted that this is the way life is. I know it isn't always that way, now. Accept a 'Thank you' from me to you, please!

I've enjoyed all the things I've ever done. Even those things I should have done better.

That summer before the war was absolutely wizard. I should have spent more time with you and less time sailing. But you'll forgive me for that, I know, because you liked sailing, too.

I think there's over a hundred pounds in the bank at Innellan, another forty or so in the Hong Kong and Shanghai Bank of Singapore, and maybe the Army will chip in what pay I have coming to me.

Take it and have a good holiday in the South of England. Stay at a hotel where your breakfast will be served in bed. You'll make me happy if you do this.

There's a great deal of good about life that will never die. There's a goodness at the heart of it, I believe.

Pass on my love to my friends, and be assured of mine for you, always. Kiss Grace and Pete for me.

Bless you!

Aye yours,
Ernest

I folded the letter to give to Tom Rigden, then I lay back on my bed of earth and looked at the scene around me. Light falling through the holes in the roof made strange patterns on the rows of bodies lying so stiffly and so quietly. It was hard to tell which were dead and which still lived. The whole atmosphere of the Death House was anti-life; over it all was the miasma of decay, the promise of nothingness.

'You too are part of this,' whispered Reason. 'There is no escape.' Yet my memory recalled me to the sanity I had known. 'The battle between life and death goes on all the time,' I said to myself. 'Life has to be cherished, not thrown away. I've made up my mind. I'm not going to surrender.'

'All right, but what do I do about it?' I asked myself.

It was a voice other than Reason that replied, 'You could live. You could be. You could do. There's a purpose you have to fulfil. You'd become more conscious of it every day you keep on living. There's a task for you; a responsibility that is yours and only yours.'

'Good enough,' I said. 'I'll get on with it.'

That afternoon I sent word to Tom that I could leave the Death House. Shortly before roll-call he came for me with two friends and a borrowed stretcher.

'Don't get ideas that from now on you're going to be the Queen of Sheba,' said Tom, as he jogged along. 'Last time we're going to do anything like this for you. You've got to get so ruddy well that you can carry *us* when your turn comes. Right, chaps?'

'Too right it is!' answered the others. 'This is his last time in the jungle limousine. From now on it's shanks's mare for Ernie!'

In contrast to the Death House, my new home was clean and neatly swept, fresh with the tangy smells of newly cut bamboo and atap palm. My friends had made excursions to the piles by the river-bank, 'liberating' an armful at a time until they had enough to build my shack. It had been added on to the wall of the hut where my friends slept, and sloped down from a height of about six feet at its peak. I was not shut off by myself. Through a door at the side, about four feet high, I could look out on to the life of the camp.

My bed was neatly made from bamboo split into narrow strips. Two rough, clean rice-sacks served as covering. Tom looked it over admiringly.

'Why, this place is so posh,' he said, 'you'll soon have chaps coming here from all over the camp to see how a bloated capitalist lives!'

I thought I detected a forced note of cheerfulness in his voice and wondered if he had been talking to the doctors.

The stretcher-bearers picked up my wasted frame, and, while one of them supported my useless legs, laid me tenderly on the clean bed. I tried to thank them. This seemed to embarrass Tom. He was not one for sentiment.

He had knocked around a bit. A Londoner born, he had been troubled with asthma as a young man, and as the doctor had prescribed a life at sea, he had taken up an apprenticeship with the P & O Steamship Company. He had stayed with them until he qualified as a master mariner. Then he had started a new career ashore with the Malayan Government, serving in his spare time with the Royal Naval Volunteer Reserve.

He sat down on the side of my bed. 'Quite all right, chum, quite all right,' he said. 'You ought to find this a bit better than that stinking Death House. We thought you could use a little comfort – for a while, anyway.'

Then he seemed to realize that he'd made a gaffe, for he added hastily, 'By the way, I scrounged an old bucket you can have for a head. I've got it outside.'

'My own private bathroom and everything! This is as good as a suite at the Ritz!'

'More than the Nips'll ever do for you, that's for sure.' Tom jumped up. 'Look here, old boy. It's getting close to roll-call time. I'd better be running along.'

At the door he said casually, 'I ran into one of your Argyll lads this morning.'

'Oh yes?'

'I said you could do with a bit of help until you got on your feet properly again. Hope you don't mind.'

'That's very decent of you, Tom. I expect I could use an extra hand for a bit.'

'I should jolly well think so. Don't worry. There'll be someone along to see that you get your rice and a wash.'

He went out, then poked his head through the doorway.

'By the way, roll-call is on your side of the hut, so you'll hear everything that goes on. What I mean is, you'll hear those bloody little bastards screaming their bloody heads off. It may amuse you.'

I was alone in the silence once more, a silence broken presently by the sounds of bare feet thudding dully on the ground, wooden sandals clattering and clobbering, the screaming voices of the guards and the monosyllabic answers of the prisoners. Then it was over and I heard the pleasing hum of many voices raised in conversation as men straggled back to their huts.

These were the sounds of life. I stretched back gratefully on my rice-sacks.

I don't know how long I had been lying there in that twilight state half-way between dozing and waking when I heard a polite cough. A man was standing in the doorway. He had to stoop down to look in. He was naked save for a clean loincloth. I could see a head of fair, thick, curly hair just under the top of the door. What impressed me most was his easy, friendly manner.

'Good evening, sir,' he said in a soft North of England voice.

'I've heard you needed a hand and I wondered if you'd care to let me help you.'

I could hear myself saying faintly, 'Thank you. I would. Come in.'

I motioned him to sit down beside me, explaining, 'My voice isn't as strong as it used to be.'

As he came over, I had a better look at him. Emaciated though he was, he had the fresh complexion of a countryman. I saw that he had a fine face, with kindness in it and a gentle strength.

'You don't know me,' he said with a smile, 'but I was posted to your company.'

I racked my brain. 'That's funny. I can't remember you.'

'I'm not surprised. I was with the reinforcements that arrived when the battalion was in training up at Seremban.'

'Did you join us there?'

'No, I didn't, sir. That's when the Corps of Military Police got their hands on me, and I was removed from battalion strength. Officially, I'm a military policeman, but I still look upon myself as an Argyll. I did my best to get permission to join the battalion when it was in action. But it wasn't any use. I wasn't allowed to change.'

'That's the Red Caps for you,' I replied. 'They've never been friends of the Argylls. No wonder they wanted to hang on to you. What's your name?'

'Miller, sir.'

' "Dusty", eh? That's what all the Millers are called, isn't it?'

'Yes, sir – the Dusty Millers – that's us.'

'Well then, I'll call you Dusty.'

'Certainly, sir.'

I studied him for a moment.

'Dusty, are you quite sure you want to help me?' I asked the question not knowing what to expect. His offer had surprised me, for it was so different from the attitude we had come to accept as normal. It seemed centuries since I had heard anyone volunteer to tend a sick man. 'I'm still pretty weak,' I warned him. 'There's hardly anything I can do for myself.' I was providing him with a way to withdraw his offer.

'Of course I want to help you,' he replied, with such warmth that there was no doubting his sincerity. 'I'm recovering from a bout of diphtheria and—'

'The old "dip", eh?' I broke in. 'Nasty stuff. Mine wasn't diagnosed until too late. That's one reason why I'm lying here like this.'

Dusty's eyes reflected his sympathy. 'Guess I was lucky,' he said. 'I got off easily. I'm still on light work, though. I've a night job in the kitchens, so I can be with you most of the day.'

'That's awfully kind of you. I'll try not to be too difficult.'

'I'm sure you won't. Here, let me get you settled for the night. I'll fetch some hot water from the cook-house and give you a proper wash.'

He soon returned, bearing a steaming bamboo bucket, a basin and some rags. He then proceeded to refresh me with the first decent wash I'd had in six weeks. It felt good to be clean again! He came to my legs and we both looked down at them. They were not a pretty sight. Skin ulcers had laced them with an ugly pattern of open sores, half-formed scabs and dried blood.

'Mm, quite a mess, aren't they?' said Dusty. 'I think I'd better wash them first. Then I'll clean out the pus.'

He gave them a proper soaking with hot water. After this, he took a piece of wet rag and began pressing gently against either side of the sores. He kept looking at me as he did so, expecting me to protest.

'Go ahead,' I said. 'Press as hard as you like. I can't feel a thing.'

This distressed him more than if I had complained, for the absence of pain told him how advanced my condition was.

'You have a deft touch,' I said. 'What did you do back on Civvy Street?'

'I worked with my father just outside Newcastle. He was a landscape gardener.'

'Did you like it.'

'Oh yes, I was one of the lucky ones.'

'What's lucky about it?'

'To do what you like and be paid for it. That's something these days, isn't it?'

'I like gardens,' I said, watching, fascinated at the gentle skill with which he worked. 'But only after someone else has done the hard work.'

'Most people feel as you do,' he replied. 'Actually, plants and flowers are much more interesting than you'd think if you don't know them. Each has its own character. Every one is unique. But they all need the gardener's care to help them make the most of themselves and to fight off the things that would destroy them. Yes, I enjoy growing things and I like trying to understand how and why they grow.'

With one knee on the ground, he was bent over, intent on making me comfortable. He considered carefully before he spoke. He was a man who thought what he was going to say. The clearly enunciated syllables blending with his soft voice made pleasing music. There was an air of natural innocence or goodness about him. I did not know quite what to make of him; I was accustomed to companions who were quick of tongue and temper. 'Why the devil,' I thought, 'is he so pleased to be alive?'

'Weeds,' I prompted to keep him talking. 'To me gardening has always meant weeding when I'd much rather be doing something else.'

'When people are down on their knees weeding,' Dusty laughed gently, 'they think only of the weeds and never of the flowers. I like to grow flowers, not weeds. But if I'm to grow flowers I must deal with the weeds. So I don't mind doing that.'

He paused to wring out his rag into the basin.

'I'm looking forward to getting back to my work when all this is over. Dad isn't growing any younger and one day I'll be taking over from him. There'll be a great need for gardens after the war – especially in the cities. That's something I'd like very much to do – bring gardens into the heart of towns – see greenery and flowers grow in brick and stone.'

He smiled happily at the prospect.

'That's fine,' I said with a touch of irony. 'You make your gardens and I'll come to enjoy them.'

'Fair enough,' he said placidly. 'I'll be looking forward to that.'

Dusty finished treating my sores. He produced two lengths of cloth and wound them around my legs, pulled the rice-sacks smooth beneath me, and picked up his bucket, basin and rags.

'I've a bit more to do in the kitchens, so I'll say good-night. I'll be back in the morning with your breakfast. I'll try to bring some salt to make a saline dressing for your legs. Have a good night's sleep.'

It was a gentle command.

He bent his back and disappeared through the doorway into the gathering darkness.

True to his promise he was back in the morning with a steaming bowl of 'pap rice' – rice that had been ground with a stone and boiled as a porridge. He also brought salt and set about preparing the saline dressings. As he worked we talked.

'Do you really think I'm going to get better?' I asked the question bluntly. I wanted to see what he would say.

'Of course you will, sir,' he said confidently. 'The lads have told me how fit you were when you were with the battalion. They said you didn't wear out easily. By the time you get back to Blighty you'll be strong. And there'll be lots to do.'

I turned the conversation back to him.

'And what do you have in mind apart from gardening?'

'Oh, I've plenty. I used to help out with youth work in my local church. I want to do more of that. There's something satisfying about working with people – especially young people.'

'What makes you think you'll be able to do any good?' I asked.

Dusty looked up with raised eyebrows.

'Why, when you work with people there's always good to be given and good to be received. At least I've always found it so, haven't you, sir?'

'I'm not sure that I have,' I challenged him. 'In fact, I haven't thought much about it. Perhaps you're right – but then again perhaps you aren't.'

'Believe me, the good is there,' Dusty replied feelingly.

He had finished me and was tidying up the shack. He first sprinkled water on the dirt floor, then swept it with a broom he had made from the leafy tips of branches.

'Why don't you go off for a snooze?' I remarked. 'You must be tired after your night's work. When do you sleep, anyway?'

He shrugged.

'Don't worry about me. I manage all right.'

Dusty went on with his chores, and I was drowsing on my rice-sacks when I heard a strange voice boom out, 'Good morning, sir. Nice billet you've got. I heard you were here, so I thought I'd drop around to say "Hello!"'

It was Dennis Moore of the Royal Corps of Signals. We had met when we were both at school in Greenock, but I had not seen him again until a short time before my present illness. Dennis – better known as 'Dinty' – was lounging with one arm against the bamboo wall just inside the doorway, as though reluctant to come in until formally invited. His hazel eyes were merry in a wide, good-natured face. When a man is wearing nothing more than a loincloth he can hardly be described as well groomed. Yet that was the impression Dinty conveyed, perhaps only through the neatness of his hairline moustache and his carefully brushed hair.

'A friend of mine in the Argylls happened to mention that you weren't exactly at your brightest,' Dinty said lightly, 'so I thought I'd drop by and see if I could do anything for you.'

'That's awfully good of you,' I replied. 'Meet Dusty Miller. Dusty's my nurse – since last night.'

Dusty smiled in greeting. Dinty squatting on his haunches, feet flat on the ground, native-fashion, in the middle of the floor, made himself at home.

'Maybe there's something I can do to help you get the captain back on his feet again,' he said to Dusty. 'Is there any particular time you'd like me to look in?'

'I work at night in the kitchen,' Dusty replied. 'If you could lend a hand then, that'd be fine.'

'Sure thing. I'm busy in the day on a work detail on the railway. Actually I'm supposed to be on the job right now. But the Nips sent me for a spanner and I'm taking my time about it.'

'How are you making out?' I asked.

Dinty ran his thumb along the neat line of his moustache; then he replied, 'Remember what the old lady said when she sat down on her false teeth? She said, "Oh well, things could always be worse. It might have been my real ones."'

He grimaced at the bad joke, and went on, 'I may be getting a posh job soon. I was a sorting clerk in the post office back home. I hear a mountain of mail's arrived, and they'll want to use my rare talents as a sorter once the Nips give the go-ahead.'

He stood up, and said cheerfully, 'Must be nipping back with that spanner. Chin, chin, Skipper. Be seeing you tonight.'

I expected Dinty to drop in now and then, but I had no idea from his offhand manner that he intended to make me his full-time charge. Thus began, however, a close association. No two men could have been more different than Dusty and Dinty – the former quiet, serene and gentle, the latter impulsive, full of fun, with a harum-scarum love of life. Dusty was a Methodist, Dinty a Roman Catholic; in their separate ways both men of faith. Their care and patience were successful substitutes for the medicines that were beyond my reach. No man could have asked for better nurses or for better friends. They guided me along the road to recovery.

31 May 1943 dawned like any other day. It was only after Dusty had given me a wash, and I was lying there thinking, that I remembered that it was my twenty-sixth birthday. I decided not to mention it. There was no place for birthday observances here.

That evening I was surprised to see Dusty and Dinty entering together. They were singing 'Happy Birthday' somewhat off-key but with great spirit. Wearing a grin like a proud Cheshire cat, Dinty brought his hand slowly from behind his back and held out a birthday cake. It was made from boiled rice, limes, bananas and palm sugar. I have had tastier birthday cakes in my life, but none which meant as much to me.

'Let's have a party!' I exclaimed, entering into their mood.

'It's all laid on!' cried Dinty gaily.

He ducked out and returned almost at once with a soot-blackened can.

'Coffee – hot and sweet!' He handed mugs around. 'Coffee that some carping critics might say was nothing but burnt rice. But I say this is coffee and I'll stand by it.'

They both raised their mugs in salutation and Dinty gave the toast: 'Here's to your happy birthday – and to far happier ones to come!'

I did not know what to say. Their kind and spontaneous gesture of goodwill moved me deeply. For a while I was unable to respond to the toast. Finally I whispered, 'Thanks, both of you. In Blighty we'll have the biggest and fanciest birthday

party anyone has ever seen. You, Dinty, can provide the dancing girls.'

'Oh, I can do that all right.'

'And you, Dusty, can provide the flowers.'

'That'll be right in my line.'

'You can count on me for the rest.'

Both answered simultaneously, 'That's a date. We'll be
there.'

We shook hands. We would all be there – if human wills
could make it possible.

They were two rare characters – so different, yet so alike –
the one, Nature's gentleman; the other, a gay cavalier – both
motivated by a deep faith and genuine human kindliness.

I couldn't say how or when, because it happened so slowly, but
gradually sensation returned to my limbs. I started a strict
regime. While I was still so weak that I could do it for only a
few minutes at a time, I would sit up on the edge of my bed
with my legs hanging over. I first picked up one leg and let it
fall, then the other. I could encircle each thigh with my hands.
By this time Dusty's care had cleaned up the worst of my
tropical ulcers. His massage and my exercises helped the blood
to circulate. The muscle tone returned and before long I could
swing my legs from the knee.

The time came when I was able to stand on my feet by
holding on to Dusty. One morning I found that with the help
of a bamboo staff I could propel myself in a clumsy, halting
way as far as the door. In a matter of days I ventured outside.
As I staggered along between the huts, gaunt and bony, I must
have looked like a prophet of doom. My long black beard and
loincloth might well have been the mark of an eremite returning from a long fast in the desert. Like Jeremiah, I might have
been crying, 'My grief is beyond my healing, my heart is sick
within me . . . The harvest is past, the summer is ended, and

we are not saved . . . Is there no balm in Gilead? Is there no physician here?'

Now I had further problems to face. The amoebae thrived on my general weakness and played havoc with my insides. I never had more than half an hour's undisturbed rest without having a trot – if one could call it that – to the latrine. I was determined, however, to do everything as though I were at the top of my strength. My skin ulcers and the beriberi were almost cured. I was certain that in a short time I'd have the dysentery cured as well.

What I had experienced – the turning to life away from death – was happening to the camp in general. We were coming out of the valley. There was a movement, a stirring in our midst, a presence. Stories began to circulate around the camp, stories of self-sacrifice, heroism, faith and love.

'Do you remember Angus McGillivray?' Dusty Miller asked me late one afternoon as he prepared me for my wash.

'Indeed I do,' I replied. 'He was in my company. A darned good soldier, too. I know him well. As a matter of fact, I defended him at a court martial on the charge of refusing to obey an order given him by his platoon sergeant. In my opinion he had every right to do so. It was a stupid order. But when Angus queried it he was immediately put under arrest.'

Dusty waited with interest as I continued my recollections.

'At the trial I put everything I had into the defence. Pulled out every stop in the organ. Backed every fact with reams of law: I'd studied law while I was in the Army. I was doing so well that at the end of the first day Angus Macdonald, the adjutant who was prosecuting, said to me, "You've won hands down. I'm on McGillivray's side now."'

'Did you get an acquittal?'

'No. The court acquitted him of the charge of disobeying an order, but got him on the nebulous charge of "Conduct prejudicial to good order and military discipline."'

'I've always thought it was damned bad law to have a charge as general as that on the books. Every soldier worth his salt could be convicted of it at some time or another. The adjutant admitted that it was the sergeant who should have been convicted and not Angus McGillivray. Aye, Angus was a good soldier all right. He came from Lochgilphead at the top of Loch Fyne. Fine stock in his family.'

'Was he with the battalion long?' Dusty asked.

'For the length of his service, which must be over eight years. He was on the north-west frontier of India most of the time the battalion was fighting there. But why were you asking me if I knew him?'

'He's dead.'

'Dead? How?'

For a moment Dusty could not speak. I could see that he was deeply moved. I wondered why, for he could scarcely have known McGillivray.

'It's hard to say. He was strong. In fact, he was one of those you'd expect would be the last to die. But then I suppose he needn't have died.'

'Then why did he?'

Dusty sat down on my bed.

'It has to do with Angus's mucker,' he began, 'who became very ill.'

It was the custom among the Argylls for every man to have a 'mucker' – that is, a pal or friend with whom he shared or 'mucked in' everything he had.

'It seemed pretty certain to everyone,' Dusty continued, 'that the mucker was going to die. Certain, that is, to everyone but Angus. He made up his mind that his mucker would live. Someone had stolen his mucker's blanket. Angus gave him his own. Every meal-time Angus would show up to draw his ration. But he didn't eat it. He would bring it round to give to his friend. Stood over him, he did, and made him eat it. Going hungry was hard on Angus, mind you, because he was a big man, with a big frame.'

As Dusty talked on, I could see it all happening – Angus drawing on his strength through his will and depleting his own body to make his friend live.

'His mates noticed that Angus had taken to slipping out of the camp at night,' Dusty went on. 'These excursions could have only one purpose. He was visiting the Thai villages. It was taken for granted that he had joined the black-marketeers! Angus, of all people! This shocked the others, for he was known as a man of high principles.'

As men died in the camp, it became possible for others to come into possession of objects of some value – watches, shirts, shorts, knives and so on. These were highly prized by the Thais, who would gladly pay for them in their paper money known as 'bahts', worth about one-and-sixpence each. Or they would barter for the goods, offering medicine or duck eggs.

'Although Angus's mates thought that he was trying to make a bit of money for himself, they didn't begrudge it to him,' said Dusty. 'Perhaps you can guess the end of the story. The mucker got better. Then Angus collapsed. Just pitched on his face and died.'

'And what did the docs say caused it?' I asked.

'Starvation,' answered Dusty, 'complicated by exhaustion.'

'And all for his friend?'

Dusty sat in stillness.

After a while, I said, 'Do you remember that verse from St John that used to be read at memorial services for those who died in the First World War? It went like this: "Greater love hath no man . . ."'

'Yes, I remember it,' said Dusty, nodding. 'I've always thought it one of the most beautiful passages in the New Testament. "This is my commandment, that ye love one another as I have loved you. Greater love hath no man than this, that a man lay down his life for his friends."'

Dusty stood without moving. Then he said, 'That's for Angus all right.'

'By some ways of reckoning,' I said, 'what he did might seem foolish.'

'But in other ways,' Dusty returned, 'it makes an awful lot of sense.'

He bent over my legs and began cleaning my ulcers.

During the next few days, on my visits to the latrine, I heard other prisoners discussing Angus's sacrifice. The story of what he had done was spreading through the camp. It had evidently fired the imagination of everyone. He had given us a shining example of the way we ought to live, even if we did not.

Yet, noble as Angus's sacrifice was, it was not the only one. Other incidents were now spoken of that, showed that death no longer had the last word at Chungkai. One that went the rounds soon after concerned another Argyll, who was in a work detail on the railway.

The day's work had ended; the tools were being counted, as usual. As the party was about to be dismissed, the Japanese guard shouted that a shovel was missing. He insisted that someone had stolen it to sell to the Thais. Striding up and down before the men, he ranted and denounced them for their wickedness, and most unforgivable of all their ingratitude to the Emperor. As he raved, he worked himself up into a paranoid fury. Screaming in broken English, he demanded that the guilty one step forward to take his punishment. No one moved; the guard's rage reached new heights of violence.

'All die! All die!' he shrieked.

To show that he meant what he said, he cocked his rifle, put it to his shoulder and looked down the sights, ready to fire at the first man at the end of them.

At that moment the Argyll stepped forward, stood stiffly to attention, and said calmly, 'I did it'.

The guard unleashed all his whipped-up hate; he kicked the helpless prisoner and beat him with his fists. Still the Argyll stood rigidly to attention, with the blood streaming down his face. His silence goaded the guard to an excess of rage. Seizing his rifle by the barrel, he lifted it high over his head and, with a final howl, brought it down on the skull of the Argyll, who sank limply to the ground and did not move. Although it was perfectly clear that he was dead, the guard continued to beat him and stopped only when exhausted.

The men of the work detail picked up their comrade's body, shouldered their tools and marched back to camp. When the tools were counted again at the guard-house no shovel was missing.

As this story was told, remarkably enough, admiration for the Argyll transcended hatred for the Japanese guard.

News of similar happenings began to reach our ears from other camps. One incident concerned an Aussie private who had been caught outside the fence while trying to obtain medicine from the Thais for his sick friends. He was summarily tried and sentenced to death.

On the morning set for his execution he marched cheerfully between his guards to the parade-ground. The Japanese were out in full force to observe the scene. The Aussie was permitted to have his commanding officer and a chaplain in attendance as witnesses. The party came to a halt. The CO and the chaplain were waved to one side, and the Aussie was left standing alone. Calmly, he surveyed his executioners. He knelt down and drew a small copy of the New Testament from a pocket of his ragged shorts. Unhurriedly, his lips moving but no sound coming from them, he read a passage to himself.

What that passage was, no one will ever know. I cannot

help wondering, however, if it were not those words addressed by Jesus to his disciples in the Upper Room:

> *Let not your heart be troubled;*
> *Ye believe in God, believe also in me.*
> *In my Father's house there are many mansions:*
> *If it were not so, I would have told you.*
> *I go to prepare a place for you.*
> *And if I go and prepare a place for you*
> *I will come again and receive you unto myself:*
> *That where I am ye may be also.*

> *. . . Peace I leave unto you,*
> *My peace I give unto you:*
> *Not as the world giveth, give I unto you.*
> *Let not your heart be troubled;*
> *Neither let it be afraid.*

He finished reading, returned his New Testament to his pocket, looked up, and saw the distressed face of his chaplain. He smiled, waved to him, and called out, 'Cheer up, Padre, it isn't as bad as all that. I'll be all right.'

He nodded to his executioner as a sign that he was ready. He knelt down, and bent his head forward to expose his neck.

The Samurai sword flashed in the sunlight.

The examples set by such men shone like beacons.

Our regeneration, sparked by conspicuous acts of self-sacrifice, had begun while 'Operation Speedo' was at its height, when work on the railway was in its most exhausting phase and we were at the very bottom of the abyss. At first I became aware of the change in the atmosphere in the camp only at second-hand through what I picked up on my visits to the latrine, for I was still on an invalid regime. The changes in attitude were most in evidence among the sick, for the able-bodied – or comparatively able-bodied – still went out every day to toil on the railway.

But after the bridge was completed, and the railway neared its final stages, the atmosphere changed. The Japanese grew less jittery. At Chungkai, those of us who were left alive enjoyed a brief respite from brutal pressure, lasting over Christmas when the camp was engulfed again by a flood of men coming back from up-country. This respite, brief as it was, created a climate in which our efforts to help one another and to improve our situation were able to grow and flourish.

It might be thought that, since this change in atmosphere coincided with my own slow return to health, it was a purely subjective thing, that in my earlier state of depression and weakness I had projected a jaundiced view of reality and that as this state receded I became aware of attitudes that had, in fact, been there all the time. Of course, my physical recovery did lead to my having an enhanced appreciation of the personalities of my comrades. But the transformation in the camp was no subjective matter; it was a concrete reality, showing itself not only in the heroic acts of self-sacrifice I have described, but also in many other new and significant ways.

One of these concerns pay. Pay from the Japanese had come late and was meagre, since they managed to deduct most of it for room and board, but at least it gave us a little something of our own. A fellow officer I scarcely knew stopped by my shack one evening to tell me that the senior British officer in charge of camp administration had called a conference of other administrative officers in his hut to try to effect a drastic change in camp policy. Some of the officers had realized that the pay offered opportunities for replacing selfishness with a more creative way of living.

It was first proposed that the officers agree to use part of their allowance to buy food from the canteen to give to the sick. This met with a mixed reception; some grumbled; others openly opposed it. The objections still echoed the old ways of looking at things:

'My pay's my own, isn't it? I can do what I please with it.'

'We're all in a tough spot; but I need everything I can get for myself.'

'When the chips are down it's a case of "to hell with everyone else." Too bad, but that's the way life is.'

The rejoinder was, 'We sink or swim together. We ought to realize that an officer's first responsibility is to his men, and ours are in a bad way. We've got to share what we have with them.' The opposition began to crumble. For the most part consciences had been touched. Some were not too happy about the decision, but the ruling was accepted.

Generosity proved to be contagious. Once begun, this charity soon extended beyond regimental loyalties to include any man in need. Men started thinking less of themselves, of their own discomforts and plans, and more of their responsibilities to others. Although the pay which the other ranks had to share was even less than that of the officers, they, too, found ways to give expression to their generous impulses. A couple of duck eggs could be bought through the canteen for one baht, and a duck egg might well save a life. Sometimes a detachment arriving from another camp after a forced march would have gifts of food pressed upon them.

It was dawning on us all – officers and other ranks alike – that the law of the jungle is not the law for man. We had seen for ourselves how quickly it could strip most of us of our humanity and reduce us to levels lower than the beasts.

Death was still with us – no doubt about that. But we were slowly being freed from its destructive grip. We were seeing for ourselves the sharp contrast between the forces that made for life and those that made for death. Selfishness, hatred, envy, jealousy, greed, self-indulgence, laziness and pride were all anti-life. Love, heroism, self-sacrifice, sympathy, mercy, integrity and creative faith, on the other hand, were the essence of life, turning mere existence into living in its truest sense. These were the gifts of God to men.

With these principles beginning to manifest themselves to us, we began to notice such forces at work around us. On occasions when we marched into the countryside on labour details we saw them in the actions of Christian natives, in the differences between the Christian way of life and the Oriental one.

Usually as we marched through the villages, we were treated with indifference and contempt. Thai maidens held their noses as we passed – although perhaps they were only being practical. Sometimes we encountered yellow-robed Buddhist priests going along the road with their silver begging-bowls. Our plight meant nothing to them – why should it? They were on their way to salvation by non-attachment. Humanity, with its suffering, was secondary. A man dying by the side of the road was left to die. There was no place for mercy in their philosophy.

But once we came to a village where we received a treatment so different that it astonished us. There was mercy in the eyes of those who rushed to the roadside to watch us go by. Before we had reached the end of their settlement they were back laden with cakes, bananas, eggs, medicines and money which they thrust into our hands. Later we learned that this village had been converted to Christianity by missionaries. The Japanese, who found out about their friendly behaviour to us, severely punished them for it.

A key figure in carrying Christianity to these jungle outposts had been an elderly missionary woman who managed to continue her work during the Japanese occupation. When she was finally forced to take to the jungle she was handed from one group of Christians to another. The Japanese knew of her existence and were never far behind. But, although they put a high price on her head, she eluded them. What her end was, I do not know.

These brief contacts with the outside world were helpful reminders that a saner, more human way of life still existed. No word had been said. But the message had been given.

Within the camp there was also daily inspiration. The strong and simple faith of Dusty Miller was one of them; it suggested that he had found the answer so many of us sought.

One evening, before he went off to his work in the kitchens, we were having a discussion about the horrifying waste of life at Chungkai. It seemed to me a good time to test him with the kind of disputation that had become familiar to me as a university student. As he was putting fresh bandages on my tropical ulcers, I said to him, 'Dusty – do you realize that more than twenty men are dying every day, here, and most of them are young?'

I dragged myself up into a sitting position the better to argue with him. 'Well, then, doesn't it make it all the more certain that there's no meaning of any kind to be found in a situation as hopeless as this one? When you look at the facts, isn't it hard to see any point in living?'

Dusty got up from the ground where he had been kneeling, moved his basin into a corner out of the way, and looked at me with hurt surprise. 'I'm not sure I follow you,' he said. 'I see a lot of point in living.'

I thought, 'He's taking this much too calmly. He must have his doubts as I do.' I pursued my argument.

'It's quite simple. All I'm saying is that when you examine the problem of our existence, the only thing you can honestly do is to admit, as Matthew Arnold did, that we are on earth "as on a darkling plain", doomed by the processes of nature to begin to die as soon as we are born. Isn't that what we have to face?'

'There's more to face than that, surely,' Dusty said gently, wringing out his rag, 'because there's more to life than that.'

'We may dream about love, truth, beauty and aspiration for

our own amusement,' I continued, 'to dull the ache of existence. In fact, that's about all we can do. Actually, we're nothing but froth on the wave.'

I was warming to the thrust of my logic.

'Religion and the arts are like a gramophone record we play to drown out the cries of pain from the people of the world. Admittedly, they help to numb the senses, but drugs can do that so much better.'

Dusty looked puzzled.

'No, sir, I can't believe that,' he replied with spirit. 'I don't think there *is* anything accidental about our creation. God knows us. He knows about the sparrow and each hair of our heads. He has a purpose for us.'

'Do you really believe that?' I said, studying him.

'Yes, I do!' he replied with conviction.

'Then why doesn't He do something, instead of sitting quiescently on a great big white throne in the no-place called heaven?'

Dusty considered for a moment. Then he said, 'Maybe He does . . . maybe He does . . . but we can't see everything He is doing now. Maybe our vision isn't very good at this point, "for here we see as in a glass darkly". I suppose eventually we shall see and when we see we shall understand.'

He seemed to be groping in his memory for some elusive thought. Then his face brightened and he said, 'Here's a verse I've always found to be of help. It makes us realize that God is closer than we think:

No one could tell me where my soul might be;
I sought for God, but God eluded me;
I sought my brother out and found all three –
My soul, my God, and all humanity.

'That's about all I can say,' he concluded.

As Dusty was picking up his things, Dinty Moore came in. I remarked to him, 'Dusty and I have been having a little argument. He claims that God has a purpose for all of us and that we can learn something about that purpose by loving God and man. Is that right, Dusty?'

'That's right,' Dusty smiled pleasantly. My attack on his beliefs hadn't upset him. Dinty now contributed his own piece of wisdom:

'Remember that old saying at home? "We are a' Jock Tamson's bairns and we've a' got to hang together." '

'And what's it supposed to mean?' I asked.

Dinty laughed, cocked his head and screwed up his face as if asking himself the question.

'Well, you might say it means – wait a minute – hmm – you might say it means – that we're all God's children and we've all got to stick together. How's that?'

'Pretty good, I should think.'

Dusty nodded his agreement.

'Rabbie Burns must have had that at the back of his mind,' Dinty went on, 'when he wrote, "For a' that, and a' that, It's comin' yet for a' that, That man to man, the world o'er, Shall brothers be for a' that." '

'I remember it well,' said Dusty. 'Dad was for ever quoting it.'

He bade us good night; Dinty set about making me comfortable.

Next day when Dusty returned, he said jubilantly, 'I've found it!'

'Found what?' I asked.

'A passage I was looking for – one that sums up what we were talking about last night. Here – I'll read it to you.'

He opened his Bible at the New Testament and read aloud from the letter of St John:

There is no fear in love; but perfect love casteth out fear;

because fear hath torment. He that fears is not made perfect in love. We love him because he first loved us. If a man
say I love God and hateth his brother, he is a liar; for he
that loveth not his brother whom he hath seen, how can he
love God whom he hath not seen? And this commandment
have we from him, that he who loveth God, love his
brother also.'

I lay back on my sleeping platform and let my mind dwell on
these words. There was truth in them. Both Dusty and Dinty
exemplified it.

For the first time I understood. Dusty was a Methodist —
Dinty a Roman Catholic. Yet in each it was his faith that lent a
special grace to his personality; through them both faith expressed a power, a presence, greater than themselves. I was
beginning to see that life was infinitely more complex, and at
the same time more wonderful, than I had ever imagined.
True, there was hatred. But there was also love. There was
death. But there was also life. God had not left us. He was with
us, calling us to live the divine life in fellowship.

I was beginning to be aware of the miracle that God was
working in the Death Camp by the River Kwai.

6

FOR THOU ART WITH ME

Thanks to the faithful care of Dusty and Dinty, I was now well on my way to recovery. True, I still suffered from malaria and dysentery, and my legs were weak and shaky, but I could get around with the aid of my staff. Compared with my condition in the Death House, I was the picture of health.

With my physical strength returning and with time to think things over, I decided I was too much of a spectator. I was allowing others to minister to me, and taking no part in the life around me.

I asked myself the question: Why was I on the fence? Perhaps it was because of my disappointment in being captured almost at the end of a well-planned attempt to escape. Perhaps it was my resentment at wasting the good years of my youth in prison camp when I might have been playing an active part in the world struggle. Perhaps these and other things had made me bitter. But Dusty's and Dinty's example, and the self-sacrificing heroism of Angus, the Argyll, and the Aussie had humbled me.

In this mood I saw I had to take my place with whatever was good, and begin to give what I had to offer, however small it might be. Having conquered the diseases of my body, I was determined, with God's help, to overcome the frailties of my spirit, as men were doing around me daily. Although not entirely conscious of it at the time, I was responding to the power of renewal in our midst. This was indeed a miracle, for we were without medicines; and we were devoid of the props of society that make for hope.

Were others feeling as I was? Were they, too, becoming aware that there is more to life than bread and bacon, pounds and dollars, Cadillacs and Rolls-Royces? Were we all coming out of the figurative Death House that our lives had become – out of the spiritual pit where fear, selfishness, hatred and despair are dominant?

Then Reason reasserted itself. The facts hardly warranted such an assumption. There was still nearly as much sickness as ever; men were still dying daily. 'Aren't you allowing your imagination to run away with you?' Reason whispered. 'Isn't part of the cure the wish to be cured?'

'Maybe so,' I had to admit. 'Maybe it's only that I'm getting used to my diseases and the environment. Or it may be simply that my glands are functioning a bit better.'

Then I heard the other voice.

'Perhaps all this is true. But there may be more to it than that. There may *be* a power beyond that of nature and man. Haven't you seen it for yourself – at work in Dusty and Dinty? Haven't you heard the evidence in the sacrifices of others? Possibly there is another form of healing – one that comes from the Most High.'

While I was still debating thus, an Australian sergeant dropped in one evening. We had never met before. He had a plan in mind, but it was a long time before I could get it out of him. He had been talking things over with his cobbers. Most of them, he told me, had called themselves Christians. But they had been so shaken by their experiences that they were wondering if there might not be something in Christianity after all that they had failed to understand. Now they wanted to give it another whirl. The sergeant was emphatic about one thing. His lads wouldn't stand for any 'Sunday School stuff'. They wanted 'the real dingo'.

'What's all this got to do with me?' I asked.

He came to the point.

'They'd like you to meet with them and – well – sort of lead the discussion.'

I was flabbergasted. I'd never done anything like this before. 'Surely there must be others better qualified. Why come to me?'

He shook his head with slow stubbornness.

'My cobbers think you're right for the job. They know you're a fighting soldier. Also, you've been to university.'

I wanted to reply, 'No, I couldn't possibly do it.' But I did not say so. Instead we kept on talking. The more we talked the more I felt drawn to my visitor. He was short, but broad and muscular. A boyhood spent in the copper mines of New South Wales had accustomed him to hardship and danger. Although he had no educational advantages, he was endowed with intelligence and a sturdy spirit. I was still hesitating when he happened to mention that it was he who had organized the first team of masseurs to help the paralysed. He was giving to others; did I have the right to refuse his request? Furthermore, the concern of his men must be great, I reasoned, or they would not have commissioned him to approach me.

'And if I do come,' I said, 'what good do you think it will do?'

The sergeant looked at me with intent brown eyes.

'It's as I said,' he persisted. 'Perhaps we haven't understood Christianity rightly in the past. Now we have to find out if it's absolute "dingo" or not.'

'What if it turns out that Christianity isn't "dingo"?'

He scratched his chin and looked me in the eye.

'Then we'll bloomin'-well know it ain't. That could be important, too. My cobbers and I have given this a lot of thought. We feel we've seen the absolute worst there is – right? Now we believe there's got to be something better.'

He frowned with distaste.

'You know, we got fed up with it; men kicking their cobbers in the teeth when they're down; stealing from the dying; crawling like rats to the Japs. No, sir! No matter how you look at it, it ain't good . . . It's rotten – rotten – rotten!'

'All right,' I said. 'I'll give it a try. But, mark you, I haven't the foggiest idea that whatever I can say will be of any use to you.'

'Oh, thank you!' He got up from his squatting position on the ground and held out his hand.

'Where would you like to meet?' I asked.

'You know that clump of bamboos just beyond the hospital?'

'Yes.'

'They're just above the "lats." We'll have more privacy there.'

'Isn't that down by the Death House?'

'Yes, why?'

I laughed. 'It's all part of my past. When do we meet?'

'Would tomorrow evening be too soon?'

'Not at all. I'll be there.'

After he left, I took stock of my meagre assets. One thing I knew for certain: in a situation as real as a prison camp it was no use discussing abstract philosophical concepts. Yet I could find little in my pre-war experience that promised to be meaningful. I'd had the usual youthful idealistic enthusiasms. David Livingstone had been one of my childhood heroes. Albert Schweitzer's life and work had been an inspiration to me, and at one time I had considered becoming a foreign missionary. But gradually I turned my back on such ideals and, in doing so, on Christianity as well. Its doctrines and practices seemed irrelevant and other-worldly compared with those of my rationalist friends.

The only two expressions of Christian doctrine I had encountered had left me unimpressed. The first maintained that the Bible had been literally inspired, had been dictated word for word and handed to man on a silver platter, as it were. The

Christian life was conceived as one of obedience to a set of arbitrary laws which seemed to be negative, restrictive and frustrating. They required one to abjure the world and its sins, to spend time in verbal prayer, to commit oneself to Bible study of a very literal kind, and to regard every disaster as a consequence of sin. The main theological emphasis was placed upon the death of Jesus Christ as a sacrifice made to appease a wrathful God.

What I found particularly hard to accept was the attitude of such Christians towards others outside their sectarian group. With the vehemence of basic uncertainty they regarded themselves as God's anointed and were therefore critical of everyone else. As far as I could see, they managed to extract the bubbles from the champagne of life, leaving it insipid, flat and tasteless. I liked the world and life. I liked good companionship and laughter. Any creed that necessitated not going to the theatre, not drinking, not smoking and not kissing the girls seemed not only monotonously dull but an incredibly easy way of getting to heaven. I infinitely preferred a robust hell to this grey, sunless abode of the faithful where everybody was angry with everybody else.

The other doctrinal expression seemed to hold that Christianity was only for nice people who had been brought up in nice homes and gone to nice schools where they had learned to do all the nice things. Heaven for this group was a kind of perpetual tea-party with thin cucumber sandwiches and smoky-tasting tea served in fine bone-china cups. It was all eminently respectable but rather hard on those outside the pale.

None of that appealed to me. Politics or social service — something of that sort — offered a surer and more realistic way to help solve the problems of mankind. Then there were the sciences. The rapid progress being made in that sphere indicated that man could take care of himself and unravel his own dilemma without help from a divine power, no matter how benign. Of such was the real world in which man had been placed by the evolutionary process, as the one creature conscious of what was going on. As he floated down the stream of history, he could know that the current would ultimately land him in Utopia.

Many brave worlds were being projected in those days, and mine was one of them. We had no idea how soon they would prove to be mirages.

As I thought over what I was going to say to the men, I realized that I had the advantage of starting with a clean slate. Like them, the thing for me to do was to find out as much as I could about Jesus.

Once, when I was a student, I had gone to a lecture advertised as the first of a series dealing with the person and teaching of Jesus. The series began with the Book of Leviticus in the Old Testament. It was not clear to me how anyone could learn much about Jesus from the variety of sacrifices reported there in abundance, so I never went to another lecture. From experiences such as these, I had reached the conclusion that Jesus Christ was a figure in a kind of fairy story, suitable for children perhaps, but not for men.

The logical place for me to begin now, I reflected, was with the New Testament, as the only record we have of his life and teaching. I had a Bible, an old one that had been given to me by a kindly other rank, who wished to lighten his pack as he set out for a trip farther up-country. It was well thumbed, torn and patched, with covers made from the oilskin of a gas cape. There were no references, explanations or annotations.

That Bible was all I had to draw on when I faced the group next evening in the bamboo grove. I was not a little dismayed to see that there were several dozen of them. They were waiting for me in respectful silence. But their faces said plainly, 'We'll tolerate you, chum, so long as you don't try any waffling.' ('Waffling' being the gentle art of evading the issue, or making a half-lie take the place of the whole truth.)

I began by describing my own uncertain state of grace, telling them frankly of my doubts and conflicts. When I asked them straight out if they were willing to go along with me and face up to the basic issues of existence, they said that they were. At first I felt my way cautiously. I told them something of what I had learned in school of Greek and Roman culture, of polytheism and Mithraism, of the life in Old Testament times. It did not take long to run through my superficial erudition. Silence fell; an uncomfortable silence. In desperation I asked for questions.

It was a risky thing to do. They might have ruined me, by driving me into a corner or forcing me into a contest of words in which I'd be the loser. But that wasn't why they were there. They wanted to find meaning in life, if meaning was there to be found.

They were very considerate – those cobbers. When they began to talk, they spoke freely of their own inner disturbances. They gave their honest views about life on earth, its object and the life hereafter. They were seeking a truth they would be able to apprehend with the heart as well as with mind. When the meeting ended, I knew I would be able to go on with them.

At each successive meeting the numbers grew. There were new faces, more pairs of eyes to look questioningly into mine. I kept one lesson ahead of them, as I expounded the New Testament in their own language.

Through our readings and discussions we gradually came to know Jesus. He was one of us. He would understand our problems, because they were the kind of problems he had faced himself. Like us, he often had no place to lay his head, no food for his belly, no friends in high places. He, too, had known bone-weariness from too much toil; the suffering, the rejection, the disappointments that make up the fabric of life. Yet he was no kill-joy. He would not have scorned the man who took a glass of wine with his friends, or a mug of McEwan's ale, or who smiled approvingly at a pretty girl. The friends he had were like our own and like us.

As we read and talked, he became flesh and blood. Here was a working-man, yet one who was perfectly free, who had not been enslaved by society, economics, law, politics or religion. Demonic forces had existed then as now. They had sought to destroy him but they had not succeeded.

True, he had been suspended on a cross and tormented with the hell of pain; but he had not been broken. The weight of law and of prejudice had borne down on him, but failed to crush him. He had remained free and alive, as the Resurrection affirmed. What he was, what he did, what he said, all made sense to us. We understood that the love expressed so supremely in Jesus was God's love – the same love that we were experiencing for ourselves – the love that is passionate kindness, other-centred rather than self-centred, greater than all the laws of men. It was the love that inspired St Paul, once he had felt its power, to write, 'Love suffereth long and is kind'.

The doctrines we worked out were meaningful to us. We approached God through Jesus the carpenter of Nazareth, the incarnate Word. Such an approach seemed logical, for that was the way he had come to us. He had taken flesh, walked in the midst of men and declared himself by his actions to be full of grace and truth.

We arrived at our understanding of God's ways not one by one, but together. In the fellowship of freedom and love we found truth, and with truth a wonderful sense of unity, of harmony, of peace.

I had need of all the grace and understanding I could acquire. For I had now volunteered for work on the Australian sergeant's massage team, and almost daily I was confronted by questions from the men we served that Reason alone could not answer. The massage team was doing useful work, as so many men were paralysed from the waist down, and in consequence suffered from terrible depression, fearing that they would never walk again. Our job was to try to get circulation started again in the wasted limbs.

Each of us was assigned four or five patients to care for, scattered in different huts throughout the camp. We visited our charges daily. As we massaged we listened to their woes and worries. When the opportunity came, we talked to them, seeking to impart assurance and to encourage their will to live.

Nearly all of our patients were young. Some of them were dying. I had reason then to be thankful for the eternal truths we had found during our meetings in the bamboo grove, for again and again my charges brought me face to face with the great basic problems of human experience. Nearly all of their queries were concealed forms of the Big One; 'How do I face death? Can death be overcome?'

Reason had no more to say on this subject than 'There's nothing to life beyond the fact that we are born, we suffer and we die.' Most of us were accustomed to such an answer, for it had been stamped indelibly on our subconscious minds by the many conditioning processes of the twentieth century. This may have sufficed for normal living, but for men dying away from home in a jungle prison camp it was not enough.

When an acceptable answer was demanded of me, I had to go beyond Reason – I had to go to Faith. If I had learned to trust Jesus at all, I had to trust him here. Reason said, 'We live to die.' Jesus said, 'I am the resurrection and the life.'

In the light of our new understanding, the Crucifixion was seen as being completely relevant to our situation. A God who remained indifferent to the suffering of His creatures was not a God whom we could accept. The Crucifixion, however, told us that God was in our midst, suffering with us. We did not know the full answer to the mystery of suffering, but we could see that so much of it was caused by 'man's inhumanity to man', by selfishness, by greed and by all the forces of death that we readily support in the normal course of life. The cry of the innocent child, the agony I had seen in the eyes of a Chinese mother as she carried her dead baby, the suffering caused by earthquakes, fires or floods, we could not explain. But we could see that God was not indifferent to such pain.

We stopped complaining about our own plight. Faith would not save us from it, but it would take us through it. Suffering no longer locked us up in the prison house of our self-pity but brought us into what Albert Schweitzer called the 'fellowship of those who bear the mark of pain'.

I was walking back to my hut one evening when a medical orderly stopped me.

'Excuse me, sir,' he said. 'There's an Argyll in my ward who'd like to see you. He came in a couple of days ago with a sick party from up-country. He's a young lad.'

'Does he need massage?'

'No. There's nothing we can do. He's dying. He has gangrene. It's all up with him.'

'What would you like me to do, then?'

'He's so miserable, I thought perhaps you could comfort him a bit. In any case, he'll be glad to see another Argyll.'

'Take me to him,' I said.

The long hut to which the orderly led me was crowded with new arrivals. We made our way down the row of sleeping platforms astir with the restless movements of suffering men. The orderly must have seen dozens of youngsters die. Yet this boy seemed to have touched him. About the centre of the hut, he stopped before a motionless figure. My heart constricted. The dim light accentuated the boy's youth and his loneliness.

'Here he is, lad,' said the orderly softly. 'I've brought him to you.'

Growing up along the
estuary, Ernest Gordon
from his earliest years.
became known as a sk
helmsman and strategi
international yacht rac
the Firth of Clyde.
on the crew of the B
Olympic six-metre ra
team, but they were ne
to compete because of
He raced frequently a
Singapore Royal Yach
before the fall of Singa

n the Firth of Clyde near Dunoon, Scotland, circa 1

Before World War II in an argyll uniform, 1938.

Ernest Gordon's Royal Air Force pilot's license. He joined the RAF in 1936 and survived a plane crash near London in 1937.

Captain Ernest Gordon in his Argyll & ...rs uniform, 1941. Photograph taken in

...middle) enjoys a relaxed moment with ... fellow Argyll & Sutherland Highlande...

Captain Ernest Gordon leading troops down to a beach in Port Dickson, Malaya, in 1941 before the fall of Singapore.

Captain Ernest Gordon carrying G.O.C. Arthur Percival to a boat in En Rompin, Malaya, Augu 1941. In February 1942 General Percival surren his soldiers to the Japan in Britain's most humil defeat of the war.

Ernest (centre) with two British soldiers circa 1940 in Port Said, Egypt, while on their way to Singapore.

The infamous 'Death Railway' extended approximately 250 miles cutting through what has been called the most inhospitable terrain in the world. It was finished in less than twelve months.

IMPERIAL JAPANESE ARMY

Date 15ᵗ JAN. 1944.

Your mails ~~(and~~ ~~)~~ are received with thanks.
My health is (good, ~~usual, poor~~).
~~I am ill in hospital.~~
~~I am working for pay~~ (I am paid monthly salary).
I am not working.
My best regards to MOTHER, SALLY, AUNTS, MRS. ARCHIE
NICOLSON, THE CHURCH AND ALL MY FRIENDS.

Yours ever,
Ernest.

Above: Postcard dated 15 January 1944 sent to Ernest's father, James Gordon. This postcard was the only kind of correspondence allowed by the Japanese, and the information was false — Ernest was not in good health, nor was he paid a 'monthly salary' for the slave labour he was forced to perform.

Below: Sketch by Ronald Searle dated 15 September 1943. The living skeletons depicted in this drawing were victims of cholera. They were British POWs held in Tarso, Thailand, one of the camps along the Death Railway. (Courtesy Ronald Searle Estate)

Allied War Cemetery at Chungkai, Thailand.

Going home after the war, 1945. Ernest Gordon (far left), en route from Rangoon to Liverpool on board the MS Boisserain with other former POWs.

...est Gordon (seated) greeting Nagase Takashi, a for...
...cer in the Japanese army. On 4 February 2000, they...
...in a ceremony of reconciliation on the banks of the...
Kwai River beside the infamous bridge.

...rnest Gordon returns to the River Kwai, Thailand,...
...February 2000. He is standing at a spot on the rive...
near Tarsau, a former POW camp.

st Gordon takes a moment to reflect while sitting ir
e of a cave in Wampo, Thailand. He is looking out
ction of viaduct on the Railway of Death where m
of his comrades died. (February 2000)

Large, frightened grey eyes stared up at me from an emaciated face. As I bent closer, he seemed to recognize me.

'Oh, I'm glad to see you, sir.'

He managed to sit up.

'I'm glad to see *you*,' I replied.

'You probably don't know me,' he said. 'I arrived with the last draft. I've seen you often, but you probably haven't seen me.'

I remembered the last draft only too well. Those who had been sent to us were boys of eighteen, with but half a year's training, and with school or apprenticeship only months behind. They were plunged into the bloodiest of actions, and the survivors experienced the worst kind of imprisonment.

The boy began to speak rapidly, as though a great weight had been lifted from him.

'I've been so lonely. I don't know anyone here. It's been a long time since I've seen an Argyll.'

'You're looking at one now,' I said, smiling. 'And there are others. You'll find friends here.'

I sat down on the narrow edge of his sleeping platform.

'It's been hard for you, hasn't it?'

'Awfully hard,' he nodded without self-consciousness. 'I've become terribly depressed, because I'm scared – I suppose. I'm so scared at times that I can't think.'

'What are you scared of?'

'All kinds of things – scared about the Nips – and scared that I'm going to die.'

What could I say? I knew that he hadn't a chance, because of the advanced nature of his gangrene. I looked at him, lying there so lonely and so young, and said the only thing I could think of: 'We'll help you not to be scared. We'll stay by you.'

This seemed to ease his mind.

'Thank you sir,' he said. 'That's good to know.'

He gave me an engaging boyish smile. I got up.

'Go to sleep now. I'll look in on you tomorrow.'

I did what I could for him, but it hurt because it was so little. I passed the word on to Dusty and Dinty; they went to see him often, and encouraged their friends to do so, too. Soon the lad had a chain of regular visitors, so that he did not spend too many hours alone.

I had been able to lay hands on some delicacies for him – a duck egg and half a hand of bananas – I went to take these to him.

'How are things tonight?' I asked.

I was delighted at the change in his manner. He seemed relaxed and almost cheerful.

'Not too bad,' he said, sitting up. 'You've no idea what a help it is to have friends. I don't feel lonely any more. And I'm not scared.'

He smiled up at me trustingly. Then, very softly, he said, 'I'm going to die, aren't I?'

I cleared my throat, searching for words. 'That's a possibility we all have to face. I've faced it – so have a lot of others.'

'I know,' the boy nodded. 'That's why I like to talk to you. You've been through it. You understand.'

I did not answer. I was thinking to myself, 'Do I? Do I? Can I ever understand even a little of what goes on in another's mind and heart?'

His tremulous smile was fading. A frown of worry wrinkled his forehead as he looked at me.

'My mother and dad will miss me. I'm the only one they've got and they'll be so lonely when I don't come back.' He sighed. 'It's tough to be young and have to die. I don't even know what this war is all about.'

'Here, let me read you something that may help.' I spoke the words evenly, pretending to be more in control of my emotions that I actually was.

I had brought my Bible with me. I opened its torn pages and

in the dim light of the hut I began to read those words that had comforted countless souls before him: ' "Yea, though I walk through the valley of the shadow of death, I will fear no evil; for thou art with me; thy rod and thy staff they comfort me." '

I looked over at him. He was lying quietly. I turned to another passage: ' "I am the resurrection and the life; he that believeth in me, though he were dead, yet shall he live. And whosoever liveth and believeth in me shall never die. Believest thou this?" '

I put the Bible down. His grey eyes were far away and he was listening within himself – to the message those words had brought. After a bit he turned his gaze to mine and said with perfect calm, 'Everything is going to be all right.'

'Yes,' I nodded. 'Everything is going to be all right.'

He slumped back. His efforts had exhausted him. I knelt beside his sleeping-platform and gently stroked his forehead with my fingers until he fell into a deep, untroubled sleep.

Two evenings later, as I was on my way to visit him again, I saw the orderly running towards me.

'Come quickly!' he cried. 'He hasn't long to go.'

Together we ran. The boy was lying without moving.

'Hello, son,' I said. At the sound of my voice he turned his head towards me.

'Hello, sir. I'm glad you're here.'

I knelt beside him and took his pathetically thin hand in mine. A yellow glow lighted the darkness behind me. The thoughtful orderly had produced a coconut-oil lamp.

'Light,' said the boy in a low voice. 'It's good to have light. I don't like the dark.'

The flickering flame rose and fell, then burned steadily, holding the shadows at bay.

'It's all right. I'm glad it's all right,' he whispered. There was a look of trust and hope on his face as he said this.

'Yes, son, it's all right,' I assured him. 'God our Father is with us. He is very near.'

'I know He is.' The sigh the boy gave was not sad, but confident.

Still holding his hand, I prayed, ' "Our Father, which art in heaven, hallowed be thy name . . ." '

His eyes were closed. But as I watched his face I could see his lips repeating the words with me: ' ". . . Thy kingdom come . . ." '

The flame of the lamp spluttered, almost went out, then seemed to burn more brightly.

' ". . . Thy will be done in earth, as it is in heaven . . ." '

His lips no longer moved. His breath started coming in great sobbing gasps. They ceased. He was quiet – with the quietness of death.

'Father,' I prayed, 'receive this dear child. Welcome him with thy love for the sake of Jesus Christ, our Saviour, thy Son. Amen.'

I put down his hand by his side, smoothed his hair and wiped from his forehead one of my tears.

His was not an isolated case. All those lads who stood faltering at death's doorway felt keenly the tragedy of dying young.

At this time, some verses came into my possession. They were written by one of them, an unknown English youth, in Singapore. His lines express what many others also felt:

What shall I think when I am called to die?
Shall I not find too soon my life has ended?
The years, too quickly, have hastened by
With so little done of all that I'd intended.

There were so many things I'd meant to try,
So many contests I had hoped to win;
And, lo, the end approaches just as I
Was thinking of preparing to begin.

It was experiences such as these that made our discussions meaningful. We were developing a keener insight into life and its complexities. We were learning what it means to be alive — to be human. As we became more aware of our responsibility to God the Father, we realized that we were put into this world not to be served but to serve. This truth touched and influenced many of us to some degree — even some of those who shunned any religious quest. Men began to smile — even to laugh — and to sing.

I was hobbling back to my shack after a rather late discussion session. Passing one of the huts I stopped. There was a sound of men singing. As I listened, I recognized 'Jerusalem the Golden'. Someone was beating time on a piece of tin with a stick. The words of the old hymn seemed symbolic to me as they rose in the still night. Maybe Jerusalem, the Kingdom of God, is here after all, 'with milk and honey blest'. Maybe man shall 'not live by bread alone'. Maybe there is the milk and honey of the spirit that puts hope into a man's eyes and a song on his lips.

They went on as I stood there, singing the hymn once more. The song made the darkness seem almost friendly. In the difference between this joyful sound and the joyless stillness of months past was the difference between life and death. This hymn had the sound of victory. To me it said, 'Man need never be so defeated that he cannot do anything. Weak, sick, broken in body, far from home, and alone in a strange land, he can sing! He can worship!'

The resurgence of life increased. It grew and leavened much of the camp, expressing itself in men's increased concern for their neighbours.

For instance, the most forlorn and dispirited among the bedridden were the amputees. The loss of legs was common amongst us — the end result of tropical ulcers and the many diseases stemming from malnutrition. Amputation —

performed often with the crudest of instruments and without anaesthetic – was often a last resort to stop gangrene and save lives.

Through our work on the massage teams we were taking some preventive measures. But those who were beyond this form of help could only lie on their sleeping platforms, unable to move about.

In one of the huts a friendship developed between a cobbler and an engineer. The engineer had an inventive mind; the cobbler was adept with his hands. They took long walks together, animatedly discussing some project. Presently they were seen working with odd scraps of material.

One day they gathered their hut-mates and disclosed what they had been doing. They had produced an artificial leg. It was a workmanlike article; the foot was a block of wood secured to a bamboo leg by strips of iron from old cans and by pieces of leather. The leg supported a round basket of leather and canvas to hold the stump. It even boasted an ingenious tin joint which enabled the wearer to bend his knee when he sat down or to lock it into rigidity when he wished to walk.

The other POWs examined it with admiring curiosity. Quite a thing. Damn' good job they'd made of it. But of what practical value was one leg when hundreds were needed? The cobbler and the engineer then offered their proposal – they would teach the amputees to make other legs just like it. With Mark One off the drawing-board, it shouldn't prove too difficult to go into mass production. It was a matter only of finding the right materials.

Thus was born in Chungkai a new industry – run by the legless, for the legless. Volunteers caught the spirit and went out scrounging for any odds and ends that could be useful. Some brought hides from the slaughter-house; others, sections of bamboo or knapsacks to be cut up into strips. Some slipped out beyond the fence at night to bring back pods of yellow silky kapok that grew wild in the jungle, for kapok was ideally suited to line the stump-supporting baskets.

When the amputees had mastered their new trade, they extended their production and made sandals for their mates who still had legs. These sandals were far from a perfect fit, but they filled their purpose of covering a man's foot, and of protecting it against cuts and bruises. Above all, they gave him a little dignity.

With mobility and work to fill the idle hours came new hope – not only for those who were able to move round the camp for the first time, but also for the many others who had been haunted by the fear that they too might lose their legs.

When I was passing the work area one evening I heard a *click-clack-thud-thud; click-clack-thud-thud*. I turned to see a cocky little man strutting proudly along on two artificial legs.

'That's quite a performance you're giving,' I said admiringly.

He grinned at me. 'You haven't seen nothing yet,' he replied. 'Keep your eye on me. When I get these pistons working properly, I'll be the fastest man in camp. The hundred yards in ten seconds – that's what I'll be doing.'

Click-clack-thud-thud; click-clack-thud-thud – it made a lively sound as he went off into the dusk.

This was the new spirit that was abroad. Along with our awakening there came a spontaneous hunger for education. Although men's bodies were frail and wasted, their minds were very much alive. To satisfy this hunger, a jungle university was established. Perhaps 'established' is too grand a word, for it was a university without lecture rooms, without colleges or halls, without examinations. Classes were held anywhere at any time.

An attempt had been made to start a similar university earlier in the history of Chungkai, but it had not prospered, being too limited in scope and intended chiefly for those who were university students or intended to be. This time the base was broader; anyone who wanted to learn was welcome. The only qualification for admission to any class was a thirst for knowledge. Enquiring students sought out their màsters among those who had had the benefit of special training and practically shanghaied them into serving as *magistri*. A group would gather around a teacher in a given subject and there they would have a seminar. As rapidly as students learned, they would put their knowledge at the service of fellow POWs by acting as leaders of other seminars. The taught became the teachers in a chain reaction.

The curriculum, for those circumstances, was amazingly varied. Courses were offered in history, philosophy, economics, mathematics, several of the natural sciences, and at least nine languages, including Latin, Greek, Russian and Sanskrit. The faculty was handicapped by a shortage of textbooks, but they were not deterred. They wrote their own, from memory, as they went along. Language instructors compiled their own grammars on odd scraps of paper.

A library was formed. It was a peripatetic library; it had no home, no lending system. Men made known the books they had and arranged by word of mouth to pass them on to others. As the library grew, the presence in camp of a surprising number of books was brought to light. The library of Raffles College in Singapore had been plundered by the Japanese, and a number of volumes from it had found their way to Changi and thence to Chungkai.

Men had clung to any books that fell into their hands – for practical reasons. They were useful for barter. The pages were prized for rolling cigarettes, for writing letters home, or for use as toilet paper. Now the situation was reversed. Books were again valued for the information they contained.

By the good graces of gifted teachers, I was able to resume the study of law I had begun in the Army. In addition I

combined the study of Greek and moral philosophy by reading
Plato's *Republic* and Aristotle's *Nicomachean Ethics* in the
original. I obtained these books through the generosity of an
Oxford classicist, whose most treasured possessions they were.

Before long I found myself teaching what I was learning to
two groups of my own. One group wanted to study elementary
Greek; the other, subjects of ethical concern. I had no Greek
grammar. By searching my own memory and that of friends, I
was able to write out an elementary working grammar on
paper scraps, which were passed from student to student. The
Japanese at that period were taking pleasure in subjecting us
during the day to prolonged roll-calls. My students made good
use of the time by memorizing the conjugations of declensions
they were in the process of learning.

My study group in ethics was no doubt typical of many
other gatherings. It consisted of three Australians, two
Englishmen and three Scots. All were as different as could be
in background and in education. One had been a professional
boxer, one a rancher, one a university student, one a labora-
tory technician, one a carpenter, one a high-school student,
one an insurance clerk and one a teacher. But all were alike in
their intellectual curiosity and enthusiasm.

In the warm tropical evenings, we met about three times a
week either at the side of one of the huts or by one of the few
bamboo clumps still left in the ever-expanding camp. Beginning with the *Republic* we discussed successive theories of the
good that had shaped the minds of people in various societies.
One in particular that provoked vehement argument was the
theory of utilitarianism.

'Blimey,' said one of the Diggers, sitting cross-legged on the
ground, 'if efficiency is the test of goodness then we'll end up
by being part of a ruddy great machine. It's only machines that
work efficiently.'

An Englishman said authoritatively, 'But if the state has to

ensure the greatest happiness of the greatest number then it
has to be governed and administered with the maximum
efficiency.'

'Oh, to hell with that!' the Digger retorted impatiently.
'That kind of efficiency means the blokes at the top telling the
rest of us what we must do. Take our proper place in society
and all that rot. No, I'm not for it. What's goin' to happen to
the poor blokes who ain't in the greatest number? Tell me that!'

'They'll be educated, I suppose,' the Englishman said coolly,
'until they learn to respect the best interests of others.'

'Browbeaten, you mean!' said the Digger. 'The sods who
write the textbooks will try to control our minds.'

'What would you expect in an ideal society, then?' I asked.

'My freedom,' the Digger shot back at me. 'My freedom to
think me own thoughts and to live me own life the way I
bloomin'-well fancy.'

'That would lead to anarchy,' said the Englishman quietly.

'And what's wrong with a healthy bit of anarchy, I'd like to
know? I'm goin' to use some of it when I get back to tell ole
Menzies what I think of him for gettin' us into this mess.'

'If everybody did that sort of thing where do you think it
would get us?' enquired the Englishman.

'It might get some peace, that's what!' came the Australian's
voice from the darkness. 'Trouble is, a bloke never has the
chance to say what he wants. If all the blokes in the world were
to tell the bosses in government that we weren't going to fight
no ruddy more wars for them then we could stay at home and
take the ole girl out swimmin' at Bondi Beach.'

There was general laughter and a murmuring of approval.

'That's what the League of Nations tried to do, wasn't it?'
called out a voice with a friendly Glasgow accent.

'No, it bloody-well didn't, mate,' retorted the Australian
promptly. 'Damn' few of the blokes in the world ever knew
there was such a thing as the League of Nations. It was all for

them smooth-tongued bastards in spats and monkey-suits —
that's what it was for.'

'Those chaps in spats,' said the quiet English voice, 'are our
duly elected representatives.'

'Not mine, they ain't!'

I asked the Australian, 'How would you run things? Let's
hear what you've got in mind.'

'By not runnin' them,' he replied quickly. 'There's too many
blockheads runnin' things as it is. The way things are, the state
controls us by force and says it does it for our own good. The
difference between a tyranny and a democracy, as I see it, is
one of degree — the degree of force that is used.'

'But we've got to have force to preserve law and order,' a
new voice broke in.

'No, we ain't!' said the Australian hotly. 'We don't have to
live by force, see! We only think we do.'

'What do you mean "think we do"?' someone jeered.

'Blimey, we've all been told that, ain't we? That's why we
studied history at school. History was just one bloody war
after another to prove that the simple blokes of the earth have
to be kept under control by force.'

Explosive murmurs of protest interrupted him.

'Now shut up and let me say my piece,' he said in a loud
voice, and then continued quickly: 'What we blokes have to do
when we get back, see, is to say, "We've had it. No more
bleedin' force. We ain't interested in keepin' on with the old
ways." What we want is for blokes to respect each other and
work with each other.'

'And how the hell do you think you're going to do that?' an
irritated Scottish voice called out.

'By doing it — just by doing it. We talk too much.'

A sharp burst of laughter greeted this remark.

'All right — I'll give you that,' said the Digger, unperturbed.
'Me too. I talk too much. We do too little, though. We talk

about democracy, freedom, brotherhood, equality and all those words, but we don't do them, see?'

I had to interrupt, 'Wind it up, Digger. "Lights out" is almost due.'

'OK. Well, what I've been tryin' to say is that it ain't the state we want to support, but a community.'

'What you want is communism!' a voice shouted out.

'No, it bloody-well ain't,' said the Australian indignantly. 'Communism just means being forced to do what the state wants and calling it equality. That's all it is . . . Let me finish! A community is people doing instead of yapping. It ain't saying we are equal — it's doing it so that it's real. It ain't shouting about truth — it's doing it. It ain't barking about peace — it's being peaceful. You get my drift?

'Look at this here camp,' he continued. 'A regular police state it is — run by force. Cobbers like ourselves have been trying to follow the Nips' example. That's why we've been tearin' at each other's throats. If you ask me, we might get somewhere if we had a little respect for each other and learned to share what we have.'

'Impossible — totally impossible,' said the English voice authoritatively.

'Like hell it is. It's impossible only because you want it to be impossible. When a gang of blokes stand up and show what they mean by what they do — then you'll see changes being made.'

The call of a bugle cut him short.

'You'll see the blokes executed,' said the Englishman.

We broke up. As we walked away from the bamboo grove, the Australian's final words echoed in my ears: '. . . then you'll see changes being made.'

'Yes,' I thought to myself, 'we'll see changes being made. And when we see them we'll see the Kingdom of God.'

*   *   *

Arguments like these did not take place in a vacuum. When we returned to our huts we were confronted by an environment that was all too frighteningly real.

In our university no records were kept; no degrees were awarded. Our courses did much to relieve the awful monotony; but they did much more than that. They helped us to see that our minds could work only on what they received from education, from experience, above all from faith. It was faith, I felt, that enabled us to transcend our environment, to appropriate what was good and true in our education and tradition, and thus prepare us to make decisions on matters of ultimate consequence to us as human beings.

It seemed to me that the quest for meaning in life, the religious search and the hunger for knowledge all go hand in hand.

One evening after roll-call I had an unexpected visitor. It was a prisoner named Dodger Green, a fair, slight, waif-and-stray type of man who had served with me in the 93rd Highlanders. Life had not treated him kindly. He had spent his youth in an orphanage in the North of England, where he had sorely missed the happy rough-and-tumble of a normal home. I had always felt a certain air of sadness about him – something which he tried to disguise by carrying a chip on his shoulder. He was always a good soldier, though – better than he knew.

This night he struck me as being more melancholy than ever.

'I've just arrived at this camp,' he said. 'I heard you were here, so I thought you wouldn't mind if I came over and had a chat with you.'

He said this very shyly, with his face averted and looking at the ground.

'Glad to see you,' I said, shaking his hand. 'How are things with you?'

He shook his head.

'Not so good. I had a pretty rough time up-country and had to be sent back. My prospects ain't bright.'

'What's wrong?'

He tapped a Dutch army canteen that he wore strapped above his right groin.

'My ruddy guts have sealed up and they end with a hole in my belly.'

'What caused that?'

'Ulcers of some kind, that's what it is. My guts cemented together. The docs tell me they've grown into each other in some queer way. I don't rightly understand how. The MO says there's nothing more to be done for me until we get out of these damn' awful prisons.'

He was such a picture of bleak misery that I tried to cheer him up.

'The sooner we all get out the better. It may not be too long now.'

He stared down at his feet.

'Maybe it *will* be too long for me – and others like me.'

'Come off it,' I said. 'You're past the worst. You've got to stick it out. You've friends who'll help you.'

Again he shook his head, as if to imply that someone like him could never expect to have friends.

'I'm not so sure about that.'

His long, hollow face with the high cheekbones made him look the last word in hopelessness.

'I'll stick by you,' I said. 'And so will others. We'll work out something together. Let me know if there's anything at all I can do.'

'Thank you,' he said. 'I don't think there is. But it was nice of you to say that.'

He raised his head, and held out his hand to bid me goodbye. He was going, and I had done nothing for him –

nothing to ease his path. I thought fast. How could I arouse some response in him?

'Have you anything to read?' I asked.

'No. I haven't had anything for a long time. I did have a detective story; but it was pinched from me – along with my mess kit.'

He brightened, and said, with his first trace of eagerness, 'Yes, now that you speak of it, I would like to read again.'

'I've a book I think you'd like. It's Richard Llewellyn's *How Green Was My Valley*. I've just finished it and I'll be glad to lend it to you. It's a great book.'

Before giving it to him, I slipped a few bahts – all the money I had – between the pages. Then I wished him good night.

Next day he came back to see me. Holding out the baht notes, he said gruffly, 'You left some money in the book. Here it is.'

He looked so self-righteous standing there that I couldn't help laughing.

'Surely you don't think I'm so wealthy that I can afford to use baht notes for book-markers, do you? Even those that have been printed by the Japs?'

His shoulders lost their stiffness and the strain left his face.

'No, I suppose not. Did you mean for me to have them?'

'Of course I did. Take them – and buy yourself some eggs and bananas. I suppose you know by now that there's a canteen in the camp, run by the Japs and supplied by the Thais?'

Rather sheepishly he said, 'I've no money – that is, I haven't had until now.' He held out the money again. 'I can't believe you want me to have this.'

'That's exactly what I do want,' I said firmly. 'Sit down and give me your crack.'

He began to talk in a friendly fashion. The more he talked the more he seemed at home in my little shack. He was sitting beside me now with his two hands round his left knee, pressing it close to his chest. After a time, he said, 'You know, I haven't had much of an education, but I get to thinking about things every now and then. I've never been able to talk to anyone about them before. I'd like to. Do you mind if I come to you?'

It had been an effort for him to make this request. He had a wistful yet hopeful look.

'Certainly not,' I replied, thankful he asked me. 'I'll be delighted to discuss things with you. We'll begin with the book you're reading and go on from there.'

We had many talks after that. First, we discussed literature in general; we spoke of authors and what they were trying to say; the symbols they used to convey deeper meanings; and the subjective quality that made reading not only entertaining but intellectually enlivening.

We went on to talk about history and the people who made history. Gradually we came to men and women and their actions. What made them the way they were? Why did they act as they did? What was unique about man? Such discussions took us naturally into the realm of religion. Dodger borrowed my Bible, and soon he was reading the New Testament with understanding and enjoyment.

All the while, he was becoming more cheerful, more hopeful, more relaxed. The strained and frightened look faded from his eyes. He laughed more and took more interest in the company of others.

One day, he suddenly said to me, 'I'm going to look around and see if I can give a hand anywhere. I've been helping the orderlies in the hospital. But I reckon I can do more.'

Eventually Dodger found where he could be of service – in a way that was badly needed. The filthiest job in camp was to collect the used ulcer rags, scrape them clean of pus, boil them, and return them for future use. A smelly, unpleasant job it was, but Dodger volunteered for it. He seemed to get satisfaction from it. Regularly I would see him going from hut to hut, carrying his noxious can of effluvious rags, and whistling as he walked.

Observing him, I concluded that he had come to terms with life. He knew that he hadn't long to live. What he had to do was to live out the days that remained to him, moment by precious moment.

Dodger turned out to have hidden assets. He had a quick eye and a sharp mind, perhaps unsuspected by himself until he learned to use them in the service of his comrades. He had only to learn of a particular need and he would take on the responsibility of trying to supply it.

A prisoner's mess tin went missing. Dodger devised one by beating two tin cans into something approximating to the desired shape. Or he would provide a container he had carved from a section of bamboo. Someone else couldn't face the rice any more. Dodger would be seen crouched over his tiny fire with his little home-made skillet, cooking up an omelet – out of a duck egg and some lime juice. When grateful prisoners paid him now and then for these small services, he accepted the money under protest. Then he used it to buy food for those in need.

The last time I saw him, his slight figure was moving energetically along, intent on some errand for a comrade. He conveyed the impression of a man happy and fulfilled by having found a purpose.

The new hope and feeling for life among many also found expression in a burst of artistic activity. Many prisoners with initiative had earlier begun to create outlets for personal expression, in workshops, laundries, shoe-making, distilling alcohol, a brickworks and similar things. In these the Australians had taken a lead, since they were rather more used to roughing it than most of the prisoners of other nationalities.

These facilities had done a good deal to ease the lot of a good number of the prisoners. But there was still a need for different kinds of expression, and it was the artistic side of man's personality that flowered chiefly under the impact of the new spirit animating many in the camp.

The POWs could hardly have turned to the arts at a less propitious time in their lives. But under the urge to give meaning to their existence they exhibited remarkable resourcefulness. For those who wanted to try carving, raw materials were at hand; the jungle abounded in all kinds of wood, some of it beautiful in hue and texture. Those who had been able to hang on to their pocket-knives were inspired to shape heads from it.

Sketch-artists and cartoonists salvaged bits of charcoal from the cook-house fires and drew with them on odd pages torn from notebooks or on the soft white inside surface of bamboo trunks. Painters made their own pigments by pounding rocks to powder and emulsifying the powder in machine oil. For brushes they used bits of rag on a stick.

Before long enough creations of various kinds had been accumulated to justify an exhibition at the end of one of the huts. The work of thirty or forty POWs was represented.

On display were carved or sculptured heads; blueprints or pen drawings of sailing-ships; portraits of hut-mates; pictures of wives or girl friends; wry cartoons of prison life. One man did pictures of his children as he imagined they looked. One had been not more than a year old when he left home; the other had just been born. He had not seen them for three years.

The first response of the visitors to the improvised gallery was one of surprise that there should be such talent among us. The next reaction was to wonder if they couldn't do just as well themselves. Thus each wave of artistic expression set off succeeding waves.

Then there was the orchestra.

I was standing outside my hut one day talking to Bill Maclean when he saw a friend of ours, an officer in the Indian Army, heading purposefully towards us.

'What's that Jim's got in his hand?' said Bill. 'I can't believe it! It's a violin!'

A shipment from the International YMCA with an assortment of games and food parcels, had just reached the camp.

'There were six fiddles among the games,' Jim explained. 'The Nips can't eat 'em or sell 'em. So they thought if they turned the violins over to us they could report that they'd distributed the parcels. That would make it only two-thirds of a lie, which is a good deal closer to the truth than they usually come.'

Jim looked from Bill to me.

'Can either of you play one?'

Bill shook his head.

'How about you, Ernie?'

'I'll have a go.'

I tucked the violin under my chin, tested the strings and tightened the keys. I had not played one since I was twelve years old. I could see the room in my home in Scotland – the sunlight on the bright flowered wallpaper, the heavy old fashioned mahogany chairs, the thick green curtains, and my mother seated at the upright walnut piano playing my accompaniment.

Taking the bow in my hand now, I tried to remember the pieces I had once learned in what seemed at the time senseless drudgery. I played a few bars from 'O Sole Mio', then from 'The Blue Danube Waltz'. As I scraped away, I had a feeling that I wasn't getting the best out of the instrument. I noticed that Bill was gritting his teeth.

Then Jim said, 'Coo! That's ruddy awful. The Nips'll think we're castrating a tom-cat.'

'You don't appreciate good classical music, that's your trouble,' I retorted.

'That was neither good, nor classical, nor music,' said Jim.

'But why must you find someone who can play the fiddle!' I asked. Jim went on to explain that now the violins had come, there was a plan afoot to form an orchestra. The Japanese had given their permission because they wanted to be entertained.

'Takes more than a few fiddles to make an orchestra,' I reminded him.

'What are you going to do about the other instruments?' Bill put in.

'And not only the instruments,' I said. 'What about scores and all that sort of thing?'

'Norman has everything in hand,' said Jim. 'Do you know Norman?'

'Oh yes, we know him,' Bill replied. 'He's a member of our club in good standing.'

'Club?' Jim looked at us quizzically.

'The Amoebic Dysentery Club. It's quite democratic. The only requirement for membership is a bloody stool.'

With Norman at the helm, we were confident that, whatever the obstacles, the camp would have an orchestra. Norman was what the Diggers called 'a Dingo Kid'. In spite of the fact that the parasites had done their worst to him, he still had remarkable enthusiasm and drive – especially where his first love, music, was concerned.

Music was the passion of his life, and he wanted it to be his profession. But his family expected him to make money instead of music, so he had taken a job with a bank somewhere in the City. In his spare time he had been conductor of a music society in the London neighbourhood where he lived. He also played several instruments himself. Gifted with a photographic memory, he could reproduce the score of many compositions on demand, for any section of an orchestra.

Norman had already pretty well organized the brasses, Jim told us, having flushed a number of trumpets, trombones and especially saxophones from among the possessions of the prisoners. The musicians for the woodwind section were already hard at work making their own instruments. I wanted to know how on earth they had obtained the materials.

'Bamboo,' said Jim. 'Bamboo, remember, comes in all sizes.'

'But how do you go about making a woodwind out of bamboo?' Bill asked. 'The whole thing sounds impossible.'

'Far from it. In fact, we're already nearly up to full strength. I'm no woodwind musician myself, but I'll try to tell you how it's done. First you choose a bamboo with the right diameter and cut it down to the length you want. Then you put a plug in one end, leaving room for the reed. Now comes the hard part — you start boring holes with a penknife to get the right notes. So you bore and then you test with a pitch pipe — or tuning whistle, one of which has turned up in camp. You do this until you have just the note you want, d'you see?'

This accounted for strange peeping noises we'd been hearing lately from some of the huts.

'It's quite simple, actually. All you need is patience.'

Jim went on to tell us about some of the other instruments.

'One chap is making his own bass viol,' he said. 'He was able to scrounge a big tea-box. He cut the wood into strips and glued the strips together. Then he had to have the strings; but that bit was easy. He visited the Nip slaughter-house; helped himself to the cows' guts — the Nips didn't mind because they weren't worth anything — took them home and dried them on the fence.'

He waved the violin.

'And these six fiddles are a godsend to the string section. Besides, this chap brought more guts than he can use so now we'll have spare strings for our violins.'

He went on to tell us about the percussion section, which was also assuming promising proportions. The men had made five or six kettle-drums by taking old oil-barrels, hammering them down to different depths and then stretching hides from the slaughter-house over the tops. The ends of the same barrels made satisfactory cymbals.

'What do they propose to do about scores?' I asked.

'That's kind of screwy,' Jim said. 'They used all the paper scraps they could find.'

The monsoon season was coming on, the time of dispiriting wetness which we dreaded. But this year we were cheered up by the anticipation of our first concert by this motley orchestra. The date was set for early October.

It was an evening to remember. To the north of the camp was a slight rise in the terrain which made a kind of natural amphitheatre and formed the obvious place for the concert. The moment roll-call was over, we rushed to our outdoor concert hall, half a mile away. We found that our Japanese captors had already occupied the front-row seats. But no matter; there was room enough for everybody, and the men quickly took their places on the ground.

The sun had disappeared behind the green bamboo. Overhead the tropic blue of the sky was deepening. Darkness would soon be on us. Norman, wearing fresh khaki shorts and shirt for the occasion, mounted the podium. He raised his baton as a signal to begin, and the heterogeneous collection of instruments launched into their first piece.

I looked down over the slope. The men sat with their hands clasped round their knees, their heads nodding to the rhythm of the music. No orchestra could have asked for a more appreciative audience.

Norman had arranged the programme wisely. He had included music for all tastes, ranging from Beethoven's Fifth Symphony to selections from *The Mikado*. From the abstracted looks on the listeners' faces I could tell that their fancies had taken wing, and were soaring far out beyond the bamboo curtain that held us in. Noble memories, long dormant, were stirred once again, helping us on the way to fulfilling the infinite possibilities of the spirit.

The night forced itself upon us, and, with the engulfing darkness, too soon, much too soon, the concert was over. At first there was absolute silence, the expectancy of men hoping for more. Then – tumultuous applause. I glanced at my neighbour; his face was shining. 'Great! Isn't it great!' he exclaimed. The cheers and the hand-clapping in thunderous echo were proof that this was the unanimous opinion. Even the guards joined in.

It is impossible to remember now how often after that concerts were held. Once every month? Every two months? Who can say? But they became important markers of time. Whenever there was a performance no one needed to ask, 'Are you going?' Everyone was going – if he could limp or crawl or hitch along on his artificial legs – or even if he couldn't walk at all. It was by no means unusual to see a man being carried up the incline on a stretcher. In music was medicine for the soul.

One night, as the orchestra was playing Schubert's Unfinished Symphony, I was sitting on the outside of the amphitheatre, not far from the road. A sick party was being marched in from another camp. It must have been a long march, for they looked exhausted. They were bound for the cook-house for a bowl of rice, and were wearily limping past the amphitheatre when the haunting strains of Schubert's lovely music reached their ears. They turned their heads; they stopped; they sat down. The rice could wait.

While they listened, their faces came to life. When the music had ended, they rose reluctantly, one by one, and moved on. I heard a little skeleton of a man say to his companion with feeling, 'God, that was lovely – bloody lovely!'

I thought to myself as I heard this, 'Aren't there two kinds of food – one for the body and one for the soul? And of the two, surely the latter is the more satisfying?'

The music reminded us that there is always beauty to be found in life – even amid the ashes.

The orchestra remained the most important of the enhancements of life. But now others were beginning to be added. Attempts at concerts had been made early in Chungkai's history, but they had been sporadic and limited affairs that suffered from the lack of any kind of facilities. Now the Japanese granted us permission to build a stage, which made possible a variety of entertainment, from light plays and vaudeville to ballet.

A stage designer named David Ffolke, who has since become well known on both sides of the Atlantic, performed wonders in getting up the sets. He made his paints and dyes from liquid mud or boiled leaves and bark. Rice-sacks and old green Japanese Army mosquito nets did service for backdrops and flats. Perhaps we thought the costumes and décor finer than they really were, for their inspired simplicity gave our imaginations much to feed on.

Fizzer Pearson, a Londoner like Norman, directed all our plays and acted in them. The plots came out of his head. Since we had no script, there was a good deal of 'adlibbing'. Both the writing and the acting may have lacked polish, but the plays were received with the same enthusiasm with which they were produced. A unity rare in the theatre existed between audience and actors. Each understood the other. This understanding bridged the gaps in production and glossed over the rough spots in the dialogue. The plays were mostly the sort of comedies or farces that have long runs in London's West End; but they brought back the tonic sound of men laughing together. This was a welcome contrast to the long months when the sullen silence was never broken except by snarls or complaints.

Two performances in particular made an impression on me. One was the 'Dance of the Scarecrow'. It was presented to us one night, without explanation or introduction. We did not know who the dancer was, but he must have been a tumbler or an acrobat, a London music-hall performer, perhaps, of considerable gifts.

Dressed as a scarecrow, he tumbled about in time to the music, as though buffeted by the wind. His gymnastic dexterity was earning him unusually loud and prolonged applause. A man in front of me leaned towards his neighbour and said in a low voice, 'Just like life, ain't it?'

The performer was much more than an acrobat – he was an artist. Through the dance of the scarecrow he was giving such an artistic interpretation of man's condition that it brought a strong response from the audience. Sympathetic eyes followed every movement, every expression. They understood the message. The scarecrow's dancing suggested that while he was taking a beating he wasn't going to give up and lie down. He would keep on going, no matter how much it hurt.

I listened again to the conversation in front of me.

'Reminds you of Charlie Chaplin, don't he?'

'Yes, the way he keeps getting knocked down, and then bobbing back like that, as though he's coming up for more.'

'Aye, he does that. He says to you that life *is* a knock-about, but you've got to keep going. It's the keeping going that makes him human, isn't it? Whenever he stops a bit, or lies down – he's just a scarecrow. Ain't that right?'

'Sure it is.'

They watched the dance. Then the second man said, 'Queer, how he's got us all thinking the same thing, ain't it?'

'Yes, it is queer.'

'Why do you s'pose that is?'

'I reckon somewhere along the line he's come to understand that's the way life is. And *we* understand that he understands. Reckon that's it.'

'Yes,' said the second man. 'I reckon it is.'

The other performance that lingers in my memory was also

a dance, although quite different in character. This was the 'Dance of the Lotus Flower'. The dancer was a Dutch Eurasian who had performed with a professional ballet company. He volunteered to do this dance which was his speciality.

As the curtain went up, there was nothing to be seen but the lotus flower itself on the bare stage. To look at it one would never have dreamed that it was made from discarded rice-sacks and stretched on a bamboo frame skilfully painted with homemade vegetable dyes.

The orchestra went into its overture. Slowly the lotus flower opened its petals. A lissom figure dressed from head to toe in black soared out and began to dance. The shadow swept around the stage in a succession of graceful arabesques. My comrades were following with rapt attention, interpreting every move-ment, each in his own way. By their sheer beauty, the symbolic movements and gestures reached into our minds and hearts to call forth memories and aspirations we had all but forgotten.

Deliciately, the dancer painted for us a picture of hope. 'Yes, life is good,' he seemed to be saying with his body. 'Look at the beauty all around us. See it in the flower of which I am a part, in the sunlight which opens the petals and the breeze which moves me. I dance because I am a part of that beauty and because I am thankful for the mystery that is life.'

He floated back into the lotus flower, and the petals closed about him.

The orchestra faded gently out.

At irregular intervals there was community singing. We passed our requests to the master of ceremonies beforehand. Usually we asked for the songs of childhood. Among the favourites were 'Tipperary', 'Pack Up Your Troubles', 'The Mountains of Mourne', 'The Bonnie Banks of Loch Lomond', 'Mother Machree', 'D'Ye Ken John Peel?' and 'Under the Spreading Chestnut Tree'.

When the singing was at its height the requests would shift to songs of a more inspirational character: 'The Lord is My Shepherd' (sung to the simple tune of 'Crimond'), 'Abide With Me', 'Jerusalem the Golden' and 'Lead Kindly Light'.

The last chords ended, the prisoners, with spirits refreshed, moved back to their huts in a state of peace they had not known for a long time.

The leaven was spreading. We were spiritually armed with faith, hope and love. We had a will to life rather than a will to death. But our weapons could be of little value unless we wielded them daily in the service of others. In that long dark period when many of us had lived by the law of the jungle intent only on our own survival we had ignored the sick. We had regarded them as an offence. The very sight of them was a reproach, reminding us that they had left their share of work to be done by the rest.

Now, although we wanted to help, it was not easy. There were so many sick, and those well enough to care for them were so few. The Japanese had strictly limited the number of orderlies, and so much of the time of these was taken up with removing the dead that the sick had to be left, in great part, to their suffering.

Since most of the illnesses stemmed from vitamin and protein deficiency, one way we could help was to supply the sick with food other than the daily rice and the very occasional tiny quantities of meat, sugar, tea and salt that sometimes found their way into our diet. There was, of course, the canteen. But our pay was so meagre that if we could buy a duck egg or a hand of bananas once a month we were doing well.

To extend our efforts, we took our chances by going outside the fence. On the edge of Thai villages scattered along the river-bank a few limes grew wild as well as the red chillis, a rich source of vitamins. Occasionally there were bananas.

Although to be caught meant death, prisoners undertook expeditions to procure these foods for their sick fellows.

We tried all kinds of experiments. We knew that fermentation produced Vitamin B. So we let masses of rice ferment in water and used the liquid as medicine. The taste, however, was so vile that we couldn't induce our patients to drink it. From a brew of this type we learned to distil alcohol which proved invaluable to the doctors in sterilizing their instruments.

Down by the hospital we started a garden. It was small and inconspicuous, but it meant more to us than an acre of diamonds because to it we transplanted any useful growing thing from the jungle. With the help of two trained botanists, one an Englishman, the other Dutch, we were able to grow a number of plants of medicinal value. Most important was one with strong narcotic properties which was used as a substitute for normal anaesthetics.

The botanists also identified certain leaves, barks and roots growing in the jungle which also had medicinal uses. One of these was a fruit about the size of an apple, evil-tasting, dark brown in colour, but effective in bringing relief from dysentery. Dinty Moore had brought me a supply during the early days when he was nursing me. The effects of the fruit were immediate, curtailing my affliction so that I was able to enjoy a decent night's rest.

The task of our medical officers was a frustrating one. In spite of the limitations, however, they were able to do marvellous work. To practise their vocation they had to draw upon all their resources. Never had the enemy Death been more powerful; never had the tools at their command been so limited. Under the circumstances it was an art, rather than a science, that they practised. Often when a surgeon was faced with a major operation, he first had to make his own instruments, turning ordinary kitchen knives into scalpels. Sutures were made out of dried guts.

The increasing availability of alcohol for sterilizing and of narcotics for anaesthesia heartened the doctors and made them redouble their efforts to help their patients keep their hold on life. More and more men volunteered to give blood transfusions. The less sick gave their blood to the more sick, until the more sick became less sick and were able to give their blood in return.

Of greater importance than giving blood was the encouragement of patients to have faith in God. Faith undoubtedly strengthened their will to live. Without it, men often died from no visible cause. With it, they survived a multiplicity of diseases, any one of which could have proved fatal.

We recovered respect for the dead. When it became apparent that someone's end was near, word would be passed around among his friends. Every effort would be made to see that there was a good turnout. It was not possible to have a set time for funerals; the dead did not keep in that damp jungle heat; and men died at all hours.

A group of friends would gather to form the funeral cortège, wearing either a clean loincloth or a shirt and shorts out of respect. They would march behind the pallbearers carrying the deceased to his last resting-place. Later, when chaplains came to Chungkai, one of them would deliver a brief service. When no chaplain was on hand, an officer would read a passage from the Bible. Every man went to a grave of his own, with a cross to mark it. On the cross a friend would carve the facts of his life; his name, regiment and rank, and the dates of his birth and death.

An orderly method was worked out for disposing of a man's effects. These were distributed among those closest to him in his unit. A new respect for the dead had created a more dignified way of burying them.

We also regained respect for ourselves because human life had value once more. Stealing ceased; mutual confidence grew, overcoming selfishness and suspicion. It extended to the issuing of our daily rations. We knew that the cooks were doing their best and that the servers were trying to be fair.

The first acts of our recovery had taken place under the worst circumstances, at the very bottom of the abyss. The drive to finish the railway had been unrelenting; the Japanese lash was on our backs; death was everywhere. As we turned to God, we were given strength to face up to our difficulties.

One living example of faith among many was a high-spirited young private from Aberdeen, who had joined our battalion with the last draft; he had entertained us with his inexhaustible supply of jokes about his native city. When I met Jock again here at Chungkai, he was running a Bible-lending library. He had thought it up, and organized it himself. By gift, barter and the fact of death, he had acquired a large stock. His prospective readers were so numerous that he could loan his Bibles out for only an hour at a time. He would then collect them and pass them on to those next on his waiting list.

Jock had heart disease, beriberi, malaria and dysentery, as well as a host of other ailments. The wonder was not so much that he was able to stay on his feet and get about, but that he was still numbered among the living. Through his faith and his humour, both of which were very great, he not only kept himself going, but infused life into others.

A day came when no Bibles were passed around. The patients wanted to know what had become of Jock. Then we learned that he had cholera and had been taken to the isolation area. This was as good as the end. The cholera compound was a place from which very few returned. Jock was mourned by the many to whom he had brought comfort and cheer. The library service was resumed, but there was no substitute for his hearty voice and kindly manner.

Then one day he was back. Although he was so diseased that

there was hardly a healthy piece of flesh on him and so weak
that he could not stand, with his unquenchable spirit he had
survived. He was bed-ridden now, but the place where he lay
became a shrine for men to visit and come away strengthened.
Their number was evidence of how much he was beloved.

I stopped to chat with him every morning on my way to
work on the railway. He always greeted me with a smile and a
kindly word. His concern was for me rather than for himself. It
was the same for his comrades, whose stories he knew so well.

One morning when I asked him how he was feeling he
answered, 'Oh, I'm nae sae bad, sir. I might be an awful lot
worse. There's always something to thank God for. I enjoy life
and I've got good friends. And it won't be so long before we'll
be goin' home.'

He gave me a big smile as though I was the one who needed
encouragement.

When I returned that evening I learned that Jock was dead.
He had died less than an hour after I left him. His body had
given up the struggle at last. A very gallant spirit had left us.

7

CHURCH WITHOUT WALLS

I do not know when the church at Chungkai was built. Perhaps 'built' is not the right word, for it was no more than a clearing in the jungle. It had for a roof the great vault of the firmament and for its walls the forest of bamboo. There were no doors. One could enter at any point. It was all door. It was hard to know when one was in church and when one was not. I remember watching two POWs carrying a load of bamboo through the neighbourhood. As they were jogging along, one of them shouted to the other, 'Take your hat off, Jock; you're in the house of God'.

The church was a fellowship of those who came in freedom and love to acknowledge their weakness, to seek a presence, and to pray for their fellows. The confession of Jesus Christ as Lord was the one requirement for membership. The church was made up of Methodists, Baptists, Episcopalians, Presbyterians, Congregationalists and former agnostics.

Two Chinese were among those baptized. Some British troops had found them still alive after a massacre on one of the beaches by the Japanese. The soldiers brought them back to Changi, dressed them in British uniforms and equipped them with fictitious identities. They were absorbed into the life of the camp and had come on with us to Chungkai. Here they were so impressed by what they had seen and heard of the example of their Christian fellows that they asked to be admitted to the Christian faith.

So far as many of us could see, there were three definitions of the Church. There was the church composed of laws, practices, pews, pulpits, stones and steeples; the church adorned with the paraphernalia of state. Then there was the church composed of creeds and catechisms, where it was identified only by words.

Finally, there was the Church of the Spirit, called out of the world to exist in it by reason of its joyful response to the initiative of God's love. Such a church had the atmosphere not of law court nor of class-room but of divine humanity. It existed wherever Christ's love burned in the heart of man. The physical temple and the doctrinal affirmation are both necessary to the fullness of the Church – but both are dead without the church that is communion, the fellowship of God's people.

Ours was the Church of the Spirit. It was not hidden in a corner, nor off on the periphery. It was the throbbing heart of the camp – giving life to it, and transforming it from a mass of individuals into a community. From the church we received the inspiration that made life possible, the inbreathing of the Holy Spirit that enabled men to live better lives, to create improvements for the good of others, and to make kind neighbours. The fruits were in evidence around us: 'love, joy, peace, long-suffering, gentleness, goodness, and faith.'

At one end of the clearing, prayerful hands had fashioned a Holy Table of bamboo on which were placed a cross and a lamp. The cross was a simply carved piece of wood; the lamp a tin can with a shoelace as wick. A roof of atap palm protected them from the elements.

These symbols were meaningful ones to us. The Holy Table reminded us of the holy fellowship to which we belonged, a fellowship made possible by the sacrifice of Him who is Lord of the Church, and by those who followed Him as apostles and disciples. Around the common table we gathered in visible evidence of His presence with us to heal, restore and to save.

The cross pointed us to our heavenly Father and at the same time reached out its arms to include us all in an expression of the Love that will never let go.

As the lamp flickered in the tropical darkness to give us the only light we had for our service, it reminded us of the life that is 'the light of men, the true light that enlightens every man who comes into the world', the light that never fails.

I first became aware of the existence of the church at Chung-kai when the Rev. Alfred Webb invited me to help him. Padre Webb, a chaplain with the Malayan Volunteer Forces, had recently arrived from another camp. He had begun a most effective ministry, quickly establishing himself as a wise and kindly pastor to an ever-increasing congregation. He suggested that I might preach once in a while.

The Sunday evening came when I was to preach my first sermon. There were no homiletic aids of any kind. But there was the Living Word, God's testimony in the Bible, and His word for our condition. Shortly before the service was to begin, Bill Maclean handed me his Bible; it was open at these words in the twelfth chapter of St Luke: 'And when they bring you before the synagogues and the rulers and the authorities, do not be anxious how or what you are to answer or what you are to say; for the Holy Spirit will teach you in that very hour what you ought to say.'

Thus strengthened, I found the words. I preached on the parable of the prodigal son. Men came with ready hearts to the services, hearts open to receive the blessings God alone could give. Days after they would approach me to discuss a point of interest. The nature of their questions made it plain to me that the basic spiritual needs are common to all men.

Every evening a service was held at which prayers were said for the sick, for those at home, and for our daily needs. We prayed for guidance and for strength to face the ordeals that lay ahead. We needed the gift of a tranquil spirit, so we asked God for an untroubled sleep. In the security of our civilian lives, sleep was a matter to which we never gave much thought. But here it was different. Men's minds were troubled by the memory of pains and horrors that allowed them no rest. Often their screams disturbed the camp.

I remember a fellow prisoner in my hut who was dying of cerebral malaria. As he turned and twisted on his pallet he carried on a conversation with an unseen presence. He had been ordered to kill a Malay, accused of being a spy, for security reasons. His conversation went something like this: 'Of course I had to kill him. There was nothing else to do. But before I shot him through the head he looked at me, with eyes pleading for mercy. He cannot forgive me; his wife cannot forgive me; nobody can forgive me.'

He went on for hours arguing with himself in this vein. As he reached the darkest depths of the valley, he became quieter and then shouted out, 'But I am forgiven. You've given me peace.'

He was at rest, and at rest he died.

It was to calm ourselves, in the face of experiences like this, that we joined together in the closing prayer of the evening:

Oh Lord, support us all the day long of this troublesome life, until the shadows lengthen and the evening comes and the busy world is hushed and the fever of life is over and our work is done. Then, Lord, in thy mercy grant us safe lodging, a holy rest, and peace at last; through Jesus Christ our Lord. Amen.

When we said the Lord's Prayer we stumbled over the phrase, 'And forgive us our trespasses as we forgive those that trespass against us.' This was not only because some of us were of Scottish background and used to saying 'debts' and 'debtors'.

It was because it meant asking forgiveness for the Japanese. We had learned from the gospels that Jesus had his enemies just as we had ours. But there was this difference: he loved his enemies. He prayed for them. Even as the nails were being hammered through his hands and feet, he cried out, 'Father, forgive them, for they know not what they do.' We hated our enemies. We could see how wonderful it was that Jesus forgave in this way. Yet for us to do the same seemed beyond our attainment.

The first Communion which I attended was memorable. The elements were of our daily life: rice baked into the form of bread and fermented rice water. The solemn words of the fraction were said:

> Who the same night in which he was betrayed, took bread and when he had blessed it and given thanks, he brake it and said, Take, eat, this is my body which is broken for you; this do in remembrance of me.

We broke the bread as it was passed to us and handed it to our neighbour. The elements were returned to the Table, a prayer of thanksgiving said, a hymn sung, and a blessing given. We slipped quietly away into the singing silence of the night, cherishing as we did so our experience of the Communion of Saints – the Holy Spirit had made us one with our neighbours, one with those at home, one with the faithful in every land, in every age, one with the disciples.

All the while our own future was unpredictable. We didn't know what the Japanese had in store for us. But whatever happened, we knew that Jesus our leader would never fail us. As He had been faithful to His disciples in the first century, He would be faithful to us in the twentieth. In the words of John Masefield's play, He is 'let loose in the world'.

8

CHRISTMAS DAY, 1943

Christmas Day was going to be something special this year. We were looking forward to it, for the opportunity it would give us to express our feelings about the new insights we had gained. We could only hope that the monsoon rains would not still be falling as they had been on Christmas Day last year, with the skies miserably grey and the camp a wallow of mud.

I had been out of my shack for some months and was living with about two hundred others in the hut for those affected with amoebic dysentery. It was a loose kind of quarantine, chiefly for the purpose of seeing that we used separate lavatories.

A few days before Christmas, Dinty Moore came to visit me. I could tell from his manner that this was no casual call. After we had exchanged amenities, he said with a smile, 'I've come to get you all tickety-boo for Christmas.'

'What did you have in mind?' I enquired cautiously.

'I'm going to shave off that magnificent beaver.'

Sadly, I fingered the luxuriant black growth; I was proud of it.

'With what?'

'This.' He flourished a kitchen knife.

'Ground to a wafer edge.'

He produced a sliver of soap and a rag.

'Sit down,' he said. 'Let's have a go at it.'

I sat gingerly on the edge of my sleeping platform while he

worked the soap to a thin lather, rubbed it into my whiskers and went to work. He carved away my beard a patch at a time. The operation resembled some ancient Chinese torture. I was sure the skin was coming off with the whiskers. But so great was Dinty's pride in his talent and his home-made razor that I could only sit tight-lipped and say nothing.

He finished at last and, with a flourish, handed me a mirror. He had left me a fine, bushy, unswept moustache; otherwise I was clean-shaven. Most of the skin, to my surprise, was intact.

'Now,' beamed Dinty, contemplating his handiwork, 'you're ready to celebrate.'

Christmas Day dawned. Through the door of the hut I saw to my joy brilliant blue skies overhead. Already we had one welcome gift, that of glorious weather.

I looked down the hut. It was hardly recognizable. The ground was clean and neatly swept. The rice-sacks bedding had been taken out and thoroughly debugged. The scruffy walls above the sleeping platforms were garlanded with green boughs – the one note of Christmas cheer the jungle offered in abundance. Men stirred, got up and began to move about, wishing one another a hearty 'Merry Christmas'.

For once we ate our breakfast in leisurely, gentlemanly fashion. Then we prepared for church. We wore whatever was our best, although it may have been no more than a clean loincloth.

I went early to church, as I wanted to have a few moments of quiet. I sat on the ground with my back against the trunk of a bamboo. Resting on the Holy Table was a Christmas wreath someone had made from bamboo branches and jungle greens. The green wreath against the ivory-coloured split bamboo made a picture of serenity.

Others had also come for those moments of hallowed quiet and private prayer. Men entered softly. By fifteen minutes before eleven o'clock, when the service was to begin, the church was full. Some were sitting on the ground, some on bamboo benches, some on home-made stools. But most were standing along the sides and at the back or front, whichever one might like to call it. Over two thousand POWs filled the area. But the hush I felt when I first arrived remained unbroken.

Padre Webb entered wearing fresh khaki shorts and shirt, and took his place in front of the Holy Table. He prayed in silence, then he raised his head and announced the first hymn, 'O come, all ye faithful, joyful and triumphant, O come ye, O come ye to Bethlehem.' He did not need to say the words and have us repeat them after him. Those who knew them sang them; those who did not picked them up from their neighbours.

Bill Maclean, standing beside me, was singing bass and in Latin. We had been at St Andrews University together. While we sang, a picture came to my mind of the going-down service before Christmas both of us had attended so long ago. I could see the scarlet-robed students and the yellow lights of the lanterns, making a warm Christmas-card picture against the old grey walls of the university chapel.

We sang a second carol, 'The First Nowell'. Then Padre Webb gave a brief sermon on 'The hope of Christmas'. We came to the closing hymn, 'Good Christian Men, Rejoice'.

We had hardly begun singing it, when we heard the almost-forgotten wail of air-raid sirens. It rose to a shriek, then gradually died away. Far off we could hear a rumble. We exchanged glances. This could not be Japanese. We kept on singing. In the blue sky over our heads we could hear a four-engine bomber flying confidently in the direction of Bangkok. We put all our feeling into that hymn. More lustily than ever, we sang 'Rejoice!' Indeed we sang so lustily that the prison guards came charging into the church shouting the Japanese equivalent of 'Shut up! They'll hear you.'

I had known of the power of praise. But I was not aware that it could soar ten to fifteen thousand feet and be picked up by a bomber crew above the engine noise.

The padre pronounced the benediction and sent us forth in peace. We were barely out of the church when someone slapped me on the back. 'Merry Christmas, Merry Christmas, Ernie old boy!'

It was Bill Maclean, wearing an enormous smile.

'You must have been thinking the same thoughts as myself.'

'You mean – that that plane was a symbol of hope?'

I changed my pace to keep step with his, and said, 'I wonder if the crew have any idea what they meant to us. Poor blighters. They're no doubt browned off because they've got to fly on Christmas Day.'

'Probably a USAF plane taking photographs. I hope they saw us.'

'If they didn't see us,' I replied, 'perhaps they heard us, after all.'

The happy looks on the faces of the men walking near us and the loud hum of their conversation as they returned to their huts and their Christmas dinners indicated they were all having the same reaction. I remarked to Bill. 'This *is* a merry Christmas – especially when you compare it with last year.'

'Last year.' He made a face. 'That was a ruddy mess.'

'It was, indeed! That was just before I got "dip" and a few other things. It was almost curtains for me.'

Bill looked more serious. 'We're not out of the woods yet – not by a long chalk. But now there's hope. That's the thing – there's hope.'

'There's something else, too, Bill,' I said. 'There's a new spirit in the camp. Have you noticed how, with many of the men, it's "You first" now instead of "Me first"?'

Bill agreed.

*   *   *

A Lancashire artillery captain welcomed us with the confidential air of one letting us in on a big secret.

'Back from your prayers, are you? Now that you've filled your souls you can fill your bellies. We're going to have a whopping dinner! Soup made from meat and bones! Rissoles with meat in them – rice and a slice of old Thai cow. And – to top it off – Christmas pudding!'

'Who're you kidding?' Bill and I chorused.

'You know that cook we've got in the kitchen?' the gunner said, overriding our scepticism. 'The one who used to be some kind of technician in Blighty? The one who claims all you need to cook properly is intelligence?'

'Sure.'

'Well, he's invented Christmas pudding made from rice. First he boils it, see, then leaves it to ferment along with bananas, limes and palm sugar, then steams it. Wait till you taste it!'

We hurried to fetch our mess tins. We wanted to be sure to be in line at the serving-rack outside the hut when the dinner arrived to savour this miracle for ourselves.

It was the first decent meal we'd had in two years. The ration of meat was small by normal standards, but lavish by those of Chungkai. I ate slowly, enjoying each mouthful and the festive atmosphere. Then came the pudding. It was delicious. Not quite like anything I'd tasted before – but delicious. In fact, it was so good that I decided to keep mine to share with Dusty and Dinty who were coming to visit me that evening.

In the afternoon there was a Christmas pantomime. It was largely inspired nonsense, something called *Snow White and the Seven Dwarfs*, with our guards as the villains and Snow White as the spirit of innocence. The Japanese, who were self-invited guests, had no notion of the fun being poked at them and laughed and applauded with the rest of us.

Visiting back and forth began in the evening and with it the exchange of gifts. From animal skins some men had made pouches, wallets, book-markers, razor strops, or covers for Bibles. From bamboo they had carved gifts ranging from simple remembrance cards inscribed 'Christmas, Chungkai, 1943' to decorated mess bowls.

In our hut most of us had made our own lamps and shared in the purchase of coconut oil. Tonight, forgetting economy, we let them burn with carefree abandon, basking in the friendly flicker of not one lamp but two.

In our circle were Bill Maclean, Ginger Ross and a small, slight, Cockney officer whom we called the Mighty Atom, because of his enormous impudence. The Mighty Atom looked around him and rubbed his hands in anticipation, raising his left eyebrow and crooking his elbow by placing his left hand on his knee. This posture gave him a cheerful look as he prepared to disclose his secret. He leaned forward.

'Ginger's bummed some alcohol. That's what he's done – he's bummed some dear old, sweet old ale – the food of rakes and kings.'

'How?' asked Bill.

'Simple,' said the Mighty Atom with a puckish leer. 'He's a bloody vampire, that's what he is.'

Ginger was in charge of the blood-transfusion service.

'All he did was sell a pint of somebody else's blood for an ounce of the water of life – and a fair trade at that.'

'I did nothing of the sort, you Sassenach sod,' Ginger laughed. 'I merely reminded the bloke who runs the still that we were buddies.'

'Fancy anyone wanting to be a buddy of yours!' jeered the Mighty Atom with a wink.

'Oh, shut up,' said Ginger.

With a triumphant flourish he produced a can covered with a piece of rag. The Mighty Atom was handing mugs around when a voice broke in, 'Just in time for the party'.

Dusty and Dinty had arrived. I introduced them to the others, and they moved in one on either side of me to join the circle gathered around the two lamps and the can of rice alcohol. I fumbled in my pack, brought out the Christmas pudding which I had saved and divided it in two.

'Here's something to wish on.' I handed each a small portion. 'And here's your Christmas.' I gave them each two duck eggs, a hand of bananas and two bahts.

Their faces, in the warm glow of the lamps, showed astonished delight.

'This is the richness, thank you,' said Dinty.

'I hardly know what to say,' said Dusty. 'It's been some Christmas.'

Meanwhile, Ginger and the Mighty Atom had mixed a brew of alcohol, lime juice and palm sugar. They served our guests first in two borrowed mugs. Ginger, having provided the spirit, was given the honour of proposing the toast. He became solemn.

'Well, chaps,' he said, 'I'm not given much to talking like Ernie here, but I'd just like to say that I hope all our Christmas wishes come true.'

We raised our mugs and drank.

In his quiet, gentle voice, Dusty said to me, 'Quite a difference, isn't there, between the way the year is ending and the way it began?' He spoke more slowly and more definitely. 'Then, none of us thought you'd live.'

'Well, you can see for yourself how wrong you were,' I smiled. 'It's only thanks to you and Dinty and others like you that I'm here . . . So you really thought I wouldn't make it.'

'To tell the truth,' said Dusty, 'I didn't see how on earth you possibly could.' Then he added softly, 'But I prayed that you would.'

After our taste of Christmas cheer we had a mug of hot coffee made from sweetened burnt rice. That finished, we sat

holding our empty mugs, fascinated by the brave flames of our
little lamps. They spluttered and sighed, but they kept going.
Ginger and the Mighty Atom were contentedly smoking
foul-smelling cigarettes made from split paper and coarse rank
tobacco grown locally for the manufacture of nicotine. Ginger
took a last puff, and said, 'About time for "Lights Out." Let's
close with "Auld Lang Syne."'

There was no need to assent. His suggestion suited our
mood. We gazed at the flames, and with soft voices sang,

> *For auld lang syne, my dears,*
> *For auld lang syne,*
> *We'll take a cup of kindness yet*
> *For the sake of auld lang syne.*

We stood up, put out the lamps, and in the dimness of the hut
we wished Dinty and Dusty many happy Christmases. As
Dinty shook hands, he said, 'It's been a grand evening.' Then
he reminded me, 'This has been our first reunion. Here's
hoping we have a lot more like it.'

I walked with them to the door and watched them merge
into the black tropic night.

Just then the bugle wailed its sad goodbye to the day.
Christmas for that year of 1943 was over.

9

ON FROM CHUNGKAI

Christmas was the high point. From that time on, conditions in the camp went steadily downhill. Since the railway had been finished well ahead of schedule, the camps up-country were being emptied, and the prisoners who still lived were returning to Chungkai. Some still had the spark of life in their eyes, but many were expressionless. Their inner spark had been suffocated. Although they had no identifiable disease, they had come back to die. Despair had destroyed the self and the will to live. Aimlessly, they shuffled along in a grey, twilight existence, waiting for death.

Chungkai had become a transit camp to hold survivors until another project could be found in which to use their failing bodies. They came in such numbers and there was so little we could do to help those who were defeated that at first we were overwhelmed. We tried every means to reach them, but their faces betrayed no flicker to tell us we were succeeding. They seemed to have no centre left with which to hear and respond. Food meant nothing to them. The tinned milk and other luxuries which we obtained for them on the black market could not tempt them. Their appetites were gone.

They were isolated from life. Talking to them of home evoked no memories, for memory had been obliterated by fear and deprivation. With memory had vanished their identity as human beings. They had been killed in a way more fiendish than physical torture. They were dead before they stopped breathing.

Yet we did not give up. We visited all new groups as they came in to see what we could do. Sometimes we found that we could ease the lot of a comrade who still retained a hold on reality. But, in general, it was a haunting experience, for we never knew when we would encounter a missing friend or an old service companion.

Once as I passed down the sleeping platforms in a hut filled with fresh arrivals, a hand came out and gripped me. A voice said, 'Excuse me, sir, aren't you Ernie Gordon who used to be in the Gourock Boy Scouts with me?'

I recognized Ian Carruthers, a friend of my boyhood on the Firth of Clyde, whom I had not seen since those far-off days. He had an ugly jungle ulcer on his leg, but, apart from that, he was not so badly off as some. We had many a blether about old times while he was with us in the camp.

In another group I met an old service companion of mine, Sergeant MacKay, who had been captured in the jungle after the Battle of Slim River in the Malayan campaign. He had a present for me. At one point he had been sent on a work party to Port Dickson, where most of our personal luggage remained before we went into action. The Japanese had taken our belongings, with the exception of one garment of which they couldn't make head nor tail – that was the kilt. They allowed the POWs to take their pick and Sergeant MacKay recognized mine by its unusual panel design; it had been given to me by a friend who had had it from the First World War. He had carried that kilt of mine from camp to camp until at last he was able to restore it to me.

At the end of February the Japanese disclosed that Chungkai was to be disbanded and its able-bodied occupants sent to work in Japan. Parties were formed, equipped with warm clothing and despatched to Singapore for embarkation.

Afterwards, at our liberation, we heard what had happened to them. They were transported in old hulks, bought by the

Japanese in the depression years. Ships that had been built on the Clyde and sailed with pride on the seven seas became the tombs of the sons of the fathers that had built them. Prisoners of war were packed into the holds, not like cattle but like coal. There was almost no ventilation, no food, very little water and no sanitation. They were stacked on sleeping platforms built three feet above one another, the space allowed being six feet by six feet for each fifteen men. Thus confined, they had to sit cross-legged for the duration of the voyage. Once at sea, the hatches were closed and they were left to stew in their own juice.

The ships displayed no red crosses to show that they were carrying POWs. In consequence, a number of them were torpedoed by American submarines. In this way died many of our friends, including Ian Carruthers.

Thus died Dinty (Dennis Joseph) Moore, my good friend, the cheerful Good Samaritan who had cheered me and cared for me when I was in the valley of the shadow.

Chungkai, too, was dying. It was almost half-empty when I was ordered to join a party being sent to a camp for convalescents at Nakawm Paton. This was supposed to be a model camp built according to Red Cross specifications, but we looked forward to it with little enthusiasm, since we'd already had ample experience of 'model camps'.

While we were waiting to leave Chungkai, Ginger Ross came running into our hut in a high state of excitement.

'Guess what!' he said breathlessly. 'Mail is being given out tomorrow. I got it straight from the horse's mouth. Right from the lads at HQ. There's a ruddy great pile of it.'

Mail! It was not possible. In all the interminable months since I had made my escape from Singapore I had received only one communication from the world outside. This was a cablegram from a friend of mine in Chungking, China, who was Far Eastern representative for US Steel. How or why it got through

I will never know. But as to what was happening at home I'd not had a word.

I had difficulty in falling asleep that night. When I slept I dreamed of the letters that had come for me. I could see so clearly the blue envelopes addressed in my father's distinctively bold handwriting. There would be letters from my mother telling me about life at home, about what my brother, my sister and my friends were doing. At the end of each letter would be added a cheerful note from my dad, expressing his characteristic optimism. These letters were so real in my dreams that I never questioned whether I would receive them or not. I knew that I would.

We waited impatiently all through the next day. Then, a little before supper-time, there was a triumphant shout of 'Mail up!' It was the first such shout we had ever heard. Ginger had been right. At the entrance to the hut were the boys from HQ with bags of mail. Everyone rushed to the doorway. Everyone, that is, except me. I walked over calmly with the assurance that the letters awaited only my coming.

Standing at the back of the crowd, I listened to the names being called out one by one. It pleased me to see the joy on the faces of my hut-mates as they went away, clutching their letters. The mail was being handed out in alphabetical order. The G's had been called. I did not hear my name. Then came the H's, the I's, the J's, the K's, the L's and the M's. The mail stack was dwindling now. Still I waited, certain that mine had been misplaced. The S's were called, the T's and the W's. Only a few still remained; and only a letter or two was left. Then there was none.

The officer who was making the distribution looked up as he gathered together the empty mail-sacks and saw me standing alone. 'Sorry, Ernie, old boy,' he said sympathetically. 'Now that this load has got through we're sure to have another one soon. There'll be some for you then.'

'Why, certainly,' I replied as cheerfully as I could.
I walked back to my bed space as slowly as I had come.

When the time came for us to leave Chungkai in the autumn
the camp was becoming noticeably thinner and our church
services less well attended. In a matter of a year the jungle
would take over. The clearing we had so laboriously made
would be choked with undergrowth and there would be
nothing left to show that here men had suffered, hoped, worshipped and died.

One morning a trainload of empty trucks stopped on its way
back from Bangkok to Burma. With surprisingly little fuss we
were paraded and entrained. Though Nakawm Paton was no
great distance away, it took us a day and a night to reach it. At
a leisurely pace we made our way along the route we had
helped to build and across the infamous bridge over the River
Kwai.

The five-to-six-year project that was to have taken eighteen
months had been accomplished in twelve. The cost had been
fantastic in terms of suffering endured and lives lost – the lives
not only of Britons, Australians, New Zealanders and Dutch,
but also of Tamils, Malays and Chinese. A prick of conscience
must have been felt somewhere, for the appalling conditions
under which we were forced to work were officially reported
to Tojo. The only action taken was that one camp commander
was selected as a scapegoat and court-martialled for the sins of
all his colleagues. At the Tokyo Tribunal held after the war it
was said that this condoned rather than punished the crime.

The railway itself was later sold to the Thais by the British
Government for two million pounds. In time the rails were
torn up. The jungle did the rest.

Our first sight of Nakawm Paton was a pleasant surprise.
The long huts had been well constructed and laid out in
blocks. There were even some buildings made of brick and

cement. These were the cook-houses. Our sleeping platforms, stretching along the sides of the huts as in Chungkai, were of planking, not of split bamboo.

We were seeking our billets, elated with what we had seen, when nearby we heard a deafening roar. A flight of Japanese fighter planes was streaking into the air from a concrete strip alongside the camp. It circled overhead, climbed into the clouds, and was lost to sight. Then we knew: the camp had been laid out in this way so that it would be clearly recognizable from the air for what it was. Quite rightly, the Japanese assumed that our fliers would not drop bombs on their own people. This would give the Jap fighters a chance to take to the air unmolested. Again, in contravention of international agreement, they had found a way to make our bodies of value to them. We took this as an indication, however, that the Japanese were getting edgy and going on the defensive, which gave us some comfort.

Nakawm Paton was essentially a camp for the sick, filled with those who had been crushed by too much work, by disease, by too little food and too many unkindnesses, the flotsam and jetsam from all the camps along the railway. So many were sick that they were segregated according to illness. One hut was reserved exclusively for tropical ulcer cases; another for those with beriberi; still another for victims of amoebic dysentery.

One hut surrounded by a high wire fence contained the men who had broken utterly and gone insane. They roamed about in their cage, twisting their hands and making strange guttural noises and staring out at us with frightened eyes. The Japanese were afraid to go near them, and had appointed special orderlies from among the other prisoners to administer to their needs. These were the first men I had encountered whom captivity had driven mad. I marvelled that there were so few.

Farther away, behind a similar barricade, was another,

smaller colony. These were the lepers. Food and other necessities were dropped to them over the wire by means of long bamboo poles.

The atmosphere at Nakawm Paton was one of general listlessness. The men had been taken from their regimental groups, from the companionship of their friends, to be sent there; hence there was an almost total lack of community. As we walked through the huts, blank eyes stared out at us from mask-like faces. It was a depressing contrast to Chungkai, where many had recovered their spirits. Here there were scarcely enough healthy men, or even comparatively healthy ones, to make a start at improving the lot of the sick,

In some ways, however, conditions were better than those at Chungkai. There was no back-breaking toil; the only work to be done was that of running the camp. The rations were slightly improved. The administration of the camp was under the direction of a British medical officer. There was also on the staff a gifted Australian brain surgeon, Lt-Col. A. E. Coates, who had passed through our escape route on the Indragiri and was taken prisoner at Padang.

Colonel Coates performed wonders of surgery every day. He had discovered among the POWs a maker of scientific instruments, who, under his guidance, fashioned an array of scalpels for special operations. For the most part, Colonel Coates had to operate without anaesthetics, although from time to time he was able to coax some from the visiting Japanese staff doctor when the latter stopped to admire his work.

At the camp we had no such reservoir of talent as we had had at Chungkai. But there were some things we could do – or at least try to do. We could make an effort to put some of these bed-ridden, hopeless men back on their feet and arouse in them a desire to live.

Here, as at Chungkai, Ginger Ross and the Mighty Atom

organized a blood-transfusion service. Those who could do so gave blood regularly. I was among the volunteers until the medical officer told me that I had reached the limit of spare blood.

Next, we formed a team of masseurs and went to work. But we found that our patients at Nakawm Paton did not want to walk. Our first job, therefore, became that of helping them to find a reason for living. This involved the stirring of memories which they had sealed off in their subconscious in order to make existence endurable. As we rubbed their muscles we talked of home and friends. This must have been as painful for them as it was for them to walk again on their match-stick legs.

One difficult case was a farmer from Norfolk. I found him lying on his rack, dirty, paralysed, weak, without hope. I affected a hearty, confident manner and introduced myself. 'Hello,' I said. 'I've come to help you walk again.'

Slowly, very slowly, he looked up at me with lack-lustre eyes. He spoke in a dialect so thick that I could barely understand him.

''Tain't any use. I can't walk. I'll never be able to walk.'

'Why not?'

''Cause I can't, that's why. And 'tain't much good you tryin' to help any.'

His tone suggested annoyance.

'What do you want me to do, then?' I asked somewhat sharply. 'Leave you alone to rot in your misery?'

'Might as well. 'Tain't any point in walkin'. 'Tain't any point in livin'.'

He turned his face away from me.

'Come on,' I said with a lightness I did not feel. 'There must be something worth remembering. Haven't you anything – a mother, a father, a sweetheart?'

I looked down at him. He was not a pretty sight.

'I'll bet a good-looking chap like you must have been a riot with the lassies.'

No response, not even a wan smile.

'I'll bet you're even married.'

'Aye, that I am. And I've a nipper I've never even seen. But 'tain't any good. There's too much sufferin' and too much trouble for anythin' good to survive. We're licked. We're all licked. The Japs will kill us all. It's all finished.'

He stared up at me in misery.

'The Jerries will have bombed my wife and baby by this time.'

I had to dispel this fear. I told him I heard the war in Europe wasn't going as badly as all that.

'Let's get started,' I urged. 'The massage certainly can't harm you and it might do you some good. There isn't too much wrong with you. You've had beriberi, but not too badly. Now you're getting better. You've lost the ability to walk. But all we've got to do is to get it back.'

Grudgingly, he permitted me to massage him. Day by day, as I worked on his useless legs, I kept up much the same kind of conversation, reminding him how lucky he was to have a wife and son to go back to.

But he stubbornly persisted, 'How do I know I've got a home left? The Jerries might have blown it up. There's been no word to say they ain't.'

'And there's been no word to say they have,' I replied. 'Is that what you're afraid of? Or are you worried that your wife is running around with someone else? One of those damn' Yanks, for instance; or a Pole?'

'No, I ain't scared of that. My wife's a good woman. She's a teacher, a primary teacher, and she's savin' her pay so that I can buy into my brother-in-law's business. He's a grain merchant.'

'Sounds pretty good to me,' I said. 'But while she's working hard building a future for you, you're rejecting it. You don't want it. You want to die. Doesn't seem quite fair to me, from what you've told me.'

He made no reply.

'Are you scared to go back in case you don't like her any more? You've forgotten what she looks like, I bet.'

'No! No! 'Tain't it!' he burst out. 'She's right pretty, that's what she is. If I'd been able to keep my picture wallet I'd show you how pretty she is. But the Japs took it off me.'

'Can you see her?' I asked.

''Course I can see her. It's as if she was standin' here before me.'

'Isn't it as I said – you are luckier than most of us!'

A faint smile appeared on his face. He began to be interested.

'Now you're feelin' sorry for yourself instead of me,' he said with a certain amount of satisfaction.

'Indeed I am. And why not? There's no lass saving up her pay for me. Any girl friends I had will have been married by this time. With all the foreign troops stationed in Britain there won't be a girl left for any of us by the time this war is over.'

He smiled a little and I continued, 'Besides, you've got a son waiting for you. You'll be a proper hero to him.'

He raised himself on one elbow to listen more carefully.

'Dads are always heroes to their sons,' I said, 'but *he*'ll have the satisfaction of knowing that you're one. Quite a romantic figure you're going to cut when you come marching home again. You'll be slim all right – thanks to the Japs – and handsome, and you'll have plenty of ribbons to decorate your manly chest.'

I went on, giving him a portrait of himself that he could see and like.

'You won't be so bad off yourself,' he said. 'A gentleman like you should do very well after the war.'

'I'm not a gentleman,' I said. 'To be a gentleman you need

an income of at least a thousand quid a year. No, I don't qualify. I'll have to find a job.'

'What will you do, then?' ·

'Well . . . ' I hesitated. 'I thought I might buy a fishing boat with my gratuity and go into the smuggling business, running brandy and scent from France to England. Or,' I mused, 'I might get a job with the Scottish Nationalist Party, become Commander-in-Chief of the Scottish Army, fight the Battle of Bannockburn over again, give you English the thrashing of your lives, and move the King back into Holyrood.'

'We'd outnumber you ten to one,' he answered.

'Why, that leaves the odds in our favour.'

'How do you figure that?'

'It's all a matter of diet, Scottish oatmeal porridge – the Shorter Catechism and Gumption Pie. Try it when you get back. You'll be head of the grain business in no time.'

'And I'll be waitin' to pull your leg just as you're pullin' mine now,' he said with a wide grin.

At last he had come round to a more optimistic outlook. We looked forward to our massage and conversation sessions, but the time came when I had to encourage him to do a little bit more. One day I said to him, 'Well, I think I've done about everything I can for you. I can stop your massage and go on to someone else.'

'Why?' he asked in bewilderment.

'What's the use? You'll never be able to walk again.'

'Who said I wouldn't?'

'You did yourself. Lying right there. Don't you remember?'

'Well, I've changed my mind. Mebbe I *will* be able to walk – if you'll help me.'

'Do you still think we're licked?' I asked. 'That trouble and suffering and death have the last word?'

'No, I don't think I do any more. Mebbe there are things that can survive even this camp – and the war.'

'Like what?'

'That I can't rightly say. I can't exactly put it into words. I have a feelin' about it, you might say.'

'Things like – faith, hope and love, maybe?'

'Yes – that's the sort of thing I mean. Faith, and hope, and love, and things like them. I should've thought of them before, but I never did. Can't make out why.'

'Then you must think there's something to live for.'

'I reckon I do. I see that mebbe there is.'

'Now you're getting somewhere,' I said. 'The message of Easter is that God isn't defeated and neither are the riches of His Spirit. You can't chuck things like love, heroism, loyalty, love of beauty and other things like that out on the rubbish-heap. They endure – when everything else is gone.'

Slowly he answered, 'That sounds pretty good to me. Why did nobody never tell me that before?'

'Perhaps they did, but perhaps you weren't listening. Sometimes we hear only what we want to hear. One of the good things about this mess is that it's opening our eyes and our ears. When God speaks to us He doesn't do so from the storm or the whirlwind, but from the silence with a still, small voice. But that's enough to keep you thinking for a while.'

I gave his legs a final slap.

'Now get up on your feet!'

He gave me a startled look.

'What's that you say?'

'You heard me!' I replied. 'Up on your feet with you.'

He did not move.

'You want to walk, don't you? Well, that's something you can't do lying on your back. Get up!'

He saw that I meant business. Without any further fuss, he did his best to obey my command. Guiding his legs with his hands, he put his feet over the edge of the sleeping rack and placed them on the ground. Then he tried to raise himself with his hands. His legs wobbled under him like macaroni. He sank back.

'It's hopeless,' he said in a dispirited voice.

I had to admit to myself that it looked that way. But I did not let him know how I felt. 'No, it isn't,' I reassured him. 'Here, let me give you a hand.'

Taking his arm and putting it across my shoulder, I raised him to his feet. Most of his weight was borne by me. But for the first time in months he was standing – even if just barely. He lurched forward. Had he moved one leg? I couldn't tell. But I pretended that he had.

'You've taken a step!' I exclaimed.

He did not reply.

'There's an old Chinese proverb,' I went on, 'that says, "The longest journey begins with but a single step". That's what you've done. You've begun a journey.'

I held him upright for a while and eased a little more of his weight on to himself. After a time he gasped, 'I've had enough. Let me down.'

His face was contorted. He gazed at me with eyes that were almost pleading.

'Do you think – that I'll ever – be able – to stand on my own?'

'Of course you will,' I said. 'And you'll walk on your own, too. It'll be a painful business at times. You've got to make up your mind to that. But we'll have you walking in a month. I'll lay you odds on that.'

He was still sceptical.

'Tell you what,' I said. 'I'll bring you a walking-stick tomorrow. Then you'll be able to help yourself a little more.'

My estimate of a month proved optimistic. But not for want of trying. Every day I spent at least two hours with him. More often than not he was so depressed that he wanted to give in. His reviving leg muscles pained him acutely. He complained that they would not let him sleep at night. I reassured him by explaining that this was a healthy sign – a sign of returning life. But he remained dubious.

At last we reached a stage where he was ready to make an attempt at walking by himself with the support of a cane. He set out, moving rigidly, like an automaton. I followed behind, prepared to catch him. With his thigh muscles he would raise the lower leg so that he could take a step. Then he let it fall and threw his weight forward so that he would be in a position to do the same with his other leg.

As he made his precarious journey down the hut, all eyes were on him. Others lying on their sleeping platforms were identifying themselves with him. He was a symbol of their hopes. If he could do this, why not they?

One day, after he had made it for about two hundred yards, I said to him, 'Now you're on your own. I'm taking your cane. Keep walking.'

Without any protest, he handed me his staff.

Alone, he took a faltering step – another step – then another. He was walking. From that ragged crowd of watching men a cheer went up.

I saw that he was near to collapse, and ran to catch him. But at that precise moment he heard the cheer. He recovered his balance, threw back his shoulders and stepped forward, walking with stiff, yet confident precision until I told him to stop. He sat down. Sweat poured from his face, but he was grinning.

'I've done it, by gum!' he said happily. 'I've done it!'

The recovery of the Norfolk farmer was not an isolated incident, nor was my work with him by any means the only kind of service that was being rendered in the camp. Again and again the massage team encouraged men who had all but lost hope to try again, and in many cases their efforts were crowned with a similar success. Such men who did make the attempt to rejoin the world of the hopeful living encouraged others. The Norfolk man's struggle had a particular effect on his hut mates who had followed every stage in his recovery. They had listened, too, to my talks with him and from time to time had joined in.

Gradually I noticed that a few of them had started coming to our church services – one or two at first, then more. I could pick them out, sitting together as a block. When I remarked that I was happy to see them at church one of them replied, 'We weren't too sure about it at first – seeing that we weren't the church-going type. But it seemed the right thing to do. Now it's becoming a habit or something, for we like it.' With an affirmative bob of his head, he added, 'Yes, sir, we wouldn't miss it for nothing now – me and me mates.'

The hut improved remarkably in appearance. When I had first visited it, it had been squalid. Although recently built, it had degenerated into a slum, redolent of the stenches of corruption, unwashed bodies and open sores. Now I noticed a change. The planks that served as sleeping platforms were regularly taken out, washed down and left in the sun to get rid of the vermin. The hut itself was swept. Perhaps this persistent fight against dirt and the bed-bugs was the most significant indication of a reviving spirit.

Some attempts were made at decoration. There were few pictures of pin-up girls; the starvation diet had taken care of the sex urge. Instead there were pictures of apple pies, roast beef and potatoes, boxes of sweets, steak-and-kidney pies, or chocolate cakes, all clipped from pre-war magazines that had come our way. I shared with others a cutting I had found in an old American newspaper containing a recipe for angel-food cake. It began with these choice words: 'Take the whites of twelve eggs . . . ' We took pleasure in reading it aloud.

More and more, the men began to help one another. The less sick cared for the more sick. The few who could walk fetched water in bamboo buckets from the well and with good-natured

banter began to wash those who were unable to wash themselves.

I realized that I was witnessing the same saving grace at
work here that had redeemed many of us at Chungkai. In some
ways the change taking place at Nakawm Paton was even
more wonderful. Since this was a hospital camp, the hopelessness had been acute. Indeed, it had been so complete that men
did not trouble to steal from each other. So many wanted to do
nothing but die. Now there was a stirring of hope, and, with
hope, a feeling among many that life was worth living.

Those who were dying – or thought they were – failed
more rapidly because they no longer wanted to eat. We made
every effort, therefore, to tempt their lost appetites with something out of the ordinary.

For instance, a metalworker had devised a crude egg-beater
out of a tin can and a perforated lid attached to a wooden
plunger. One of our cooks had invented a confection of
mashed bananas, duck eggs and lime juice. Whipped to a
creamy froth with the home-made egg-beater and poured over
a bowl of rice, the mixture was a tasty dish.

When it was first offered, patients usually rejected it. Then
we'd say, 'Oh, come on. Old Jim got this up especially for you.
You wouldn't want to disappoint him, would you?'

The thought that someone had gone to so much trouble for
them was often more of a turning-point than the dish itself.

Men's minds, too, yearned to be fed. We were handicapped
by a lack of the variety of talent we had enjoyed at Chungkai.
But since, in view of the need, we concluded that anything
would be better than nothing, we initiated a programme of
'make-do' diversion.

Debating teams were organized with two on a side. They
made the rounds of the huts, disputing on assigned topics. A
favourite was 'Has twentieth-century man lost the ability to
entertain himself?' Another: 'Resolved: That old-age pensions

should begin at twenty-one.' When the debaters grew bored they changed sides and presented the opposite point of view with equal gusto.

On one of the teams was a debonair Londoner already giving promise of his successful future as a barrister. He had an electric personality and a gift of eloquence. One night he came to me with an idea; why not tell stories of famous trials? He gave a sample performance and proved to be a hit. So great was his skill, that as he stood before us in his loincloth we could see him in our mind's eye in wig and gown, addressing the bench.

Any semblance of talent was put to use. One prisoner gave popular lectures on 'The scientific approach to golf'. An architect conducted a course on 'How to design a house'. The kitchen and the bathroom were the two rooms in which everyone showed the greatest interest.

The sea held a great fascination for many. Some designed yachts which they could never hope to own, or attended classes on how to build and sail a small boat. Once I recounted my adventures on the *Setia Berganti* to a group in my hut. The word got around and I was asked to tell it over and over to others.

The men also enjoyed listening to selections read from books. They liked especially simple tales that evoked nostalgic pictures of living in other times. Among the most popular were the tales of Washington Irving, such as *The Legend of Sleepy Hollow* and *Rip Van Winkle*. The more the men heard of the problems, foibles, quirks, eccentricities, humours and virtues of other people, the more they regained interest in the human race and in themselves. The evening reading sessions became increasingly popular. As I read, I sat on the edge of a sleeping platform, holding my book close to the flickering little flame and giving as much feeling to the words as I could muster. The words conveyed pictures — of home, of families gathered around the parlour fire.

When I had finished my story for the night, I was aware of a sense of kinship. We were human beings with the same problems and the same hopes. We were being drawn towards a centre that was beyond ourselves, a centre that was good, that gave us cause to hope, that promised the fulfilment of life – a life that was joyously sweet.

One evening I said to one of the men to whom I'd been reading, 'A lot of the lads seem to be much happier these days.'

'Yes, they are,' he agreed. He was a small slip of a man. In years he could have been no more than twenty-eight, yet illness and suffering had given him a grey, aged look.

He reflected a moment and then said, 'Do you know what I've come to think? There's a harmony about life. When you put yourself in tune with that harmony you sense a kind of rightness about things. You know a peace in your heart.'

'Do you think you've found that peace?'

'Yes, I reckon I have. I used to gripe and complain about everything – about the Nips, the Government, my mates, myself.'

'Most of us have felt that way,' I acknowledged.

'Maybe. But I bet I was one of the worst.'

'How do you think that change came about?' I asked.

'It came gradually,' he answered. 'I learned to accept things – to accept the Nips and their awfulness – to accept my mates – to accept myself. Then I stopped griping so much and tried to do what I could to help others. Every little bit I gave made me seem more at ease with myself. I decided that, no matter what happens, I've got to do what I believe to be right.'

'And what do you mean by "right"?'

He looked puzzled.

'I don't know exactly. It means – er – not thinking so much about yourself and – er – taking time to think about what you ought to do. I've never been much of a one to pray – but that's what I'm doing. I'm praying. Prayer makes me feel stronger, see – and then I'm ready for whatever's coming next.'

'Is that what you mean by the harmony of life?'

'Yes, it is, I suppose. It's a power. When you get in line with it, you know it and you know it's right.'

'Isn't that the same thing as doing God's will?'

'I suppose it is,' he agreed. 'I never went to services before. When I joined the Army I put down my religion as Church of England. But I never went – except on church parades. Now what seems to me important about a church is that we all come together as one when we open ourselves to God's will. You carry some of the harmony away with you when you leave the church.'

'You've got something there,' I said.

'Well, I must be going now,' he smiled at me. 'I'll see you in church.'

We shook hands and he left me.

An attempt was made to start the university again, but we lacked the trained scholars we had had at Chungkai. I had smuggled in the scraps of paper that made up the Greek grammar I had compiled. We had sessions in Greek and also in ethics and philosophy.

Not many members of the Chungkai church were in this camp, but a few of us started services again in the open air. At one of these services a guard walked up to me as I was preaching, shouted, *'Curra, bagero!'* and struck me on the face. I politely told him to go away. Strangely enough, he did. Then he thought better of it, and came back to administer another slap before leaving us to finish the service in peace.

It was interesting to note that during this period, the men were unmoved by the outward observances of the Church. We realized this after we had invited a Chaplain to give a course of addresses on this subject. The first meeting, held in a corner of one of the huts, was well attended. The chaplain talked about the need to subscribe to the outward forms used by the Church, without explaining sufficiently their meaning. Most of the men went away dissatisfied. There seemed nothing for them to do; the professional would take care of everything. When the third meeting was held, hardly anybody came at all.

Not long after, some of the men asked me to give a series of talks on the Christian faith that would be closer to the interests of the majority. Once more I found myself discussing the basic issues of existence with a group that grew steadily. As I did this every night, I became limp with exhaustion. But the intense interest and sympathy of my listeners kept me going.

In our nocturnal sessions by the bamboo grove at Chungkai we had grown to know Jesus. We had confined our explorations to a study of his life and teachings. Now, those of us who had moved to Nakawm Paton were ready to proceed to an evaluation of what we had learned – both from our discussions and from our experience.

Some contemporary writers – Kafka, Sartre, Beckett and Camus among them – have been credited with reminding theologians of the sinfulness of man. This was something of which we needed no reminder. We knew all about sin. We had seen for ourselves how low man can fall.

We wanted to learn now what Christianity had to say about our redemption. Before we could do, we had to be. It was not only our minds but also our wills that had to be changed. We had to be called into being by love. That lonely figure on the Cross had redeemed mankind by His love and sacrifice. Yet while that redemption was a once-for-all event, it was also a fact that we had to be redeemed daily to be in a state of being redeemed.

As guilty men, we wanted to understand how the Christian life shared in the fate and condition of the world. Because we were men we were involved in the world with all its imperfections. We were victims of the Japanese, but we also shared their blood guilt. Like them, we had killed in battle and lived by the law of a life for a life, a hand for a hand, an eye for an eye, a wound for a wound, a stripe for a stripe. We were also involved because of our uncertainties. Not only our captors threatened us, but life itself. The props of Western civilization had been swept from under us, and with them our faith in man and the things of man – his technology, his belief in progress, his utopianism, his rationalism, his pride. With others of the twentieth century, we hung suspended over the big hole, the abyss of meaninglessness, and the outlook was bleak.

We were involved, too, because of our doubts. Some of us had turned to Christianity from unbelief and still carried with us our fear of faith. We could say with Dostoevski: 'It is not as a child that I believe and confess Jesus Christ. My "hosanna" is born of a furnace of doubt.' Our doubts were our inheritance as children of our times.

We had two alternatives: we could choose the way of men, based on the sovereignty of the natural order, closed, sealed and impersonal; or we could choose the way of Jesus Christ, free and personal, based on the sovereignty of God the Father.

The wind of the spirit had blown upon us; we could not prove how or whence it had come. But our experience pointed to a source beyond ourselves. We knew personal fulfilment, love, joy, peace, wholeness, as we committed ourselves to the One who had called us. Only as we responded to this Word did we receive the power to progress towards true humanity. Our life on the horizontal plane was made meaningful at the point where it was met by the vertical. At the point marked by the Cross we found ourselves.

Christmas was coming round again. Our third year in captivity, the year 1944, was drawing to a close. But we were no nearer freedom than the year before. The only news we had came to us from our captors, who told us that their armies had taken India and were about to join forces with Rommel in North Africa. Soon the war would be over, with the Axis triumphant. We knew this was not true. We were convinced that the conflict would end in our favour. But what interested us was whether we would live long enough to see that end. How many more Christmases could we survive?

We were determined, all the same, to make Christmas a day to be remembered, like the last one. We planned a special church service for the morning and recreation for the afternoon. A feature of the latter was to be a Derby, with the healthiest men as horses and the skinniest as jockeys. The cooks were preparing to tempt our palates with a holiday menu.

We were working hard to get things ready, when a train pulled in on the siding. We saw bloody stretchers being lifted carefully out of the railway cars. We were summoned to help carry the wounded men to the operating hut. They had been brought there from the nearby camp of Nong Pladuk. From their lips we heard the story of how, as they were lining up for their evening ration, a squadron of our bombers had appeared without warning and dumped their load on the camp. Since Nong Pladuk was located beside a marshalling yard, our fliers had apparently mistaken it for a military base. One hundred and twenty-five men were killed outright and over four hundred injured.

The surgeons made ready to operate and the blood transfusion teams stood by. For the present we forgot our Christmas plans in caring for the avalanche of wounded men. This development cast a pall over our spirits. But we were determined not to be subdued by it, and as soon as we were able, we resumed our preparations.

Christmas Day dawned warm, but not oppressive. Again I went early to church. But this time I was to be the preacher. The hut was filling up when I arrived, and soon it was packed from wall to wall and overflowing through the doors. Before me were many nationalities – English, Welsh, Scots, Australians, New Zealanders, Americans, Dutch, Eurasians.

My heart swelled at the sight of them. Their faces were gaunt, hollow-cheeked, skin drawn tight over the bones. But determination was reflected in their eyes – and courage, faith, hope and love. Gone was that empty look which revealed listlessness, fatalism, or despair. They had the fibre of men who would not be defeated whatever ordeals they faced.

Without benefit of instrumental accompaniment, we all sang together with great gusto the traditional hymns. I spoke briefly, as Padre Webb had done last year, of the hope that Christmas brings. I pronounced the benediction and the men streamed out into the warm tropic sunlight.

Once more we had our Christmas dinner, topped off with the traditional Christmas pudding. This time the performance in the cook-house impressed the Japanese. If these cooks could accomplish so much with so little, they reasoned, what couldn't they do if given a free hand? One of the officers decided to throw a party; he ordered the best cook to be sent to him for instructions. He made it clear that he wanted a super-feast, Christmas style, for his guests, and he instructed the chef to spare no pains.

The dinner that night was the last word. The *pièce de résistance* was a work of art, a large bird shinily glazed and beautifully decorated. The chef described it as the kind of holiday turkey Americans ate at their family dinners. The Japanese guests gorged themselves, picking the bird to the bone. That night a number of them became violently ill. The officer called the cook and demanded an explanation. In the Western world, the cook declared, the ceremonial fowl is viewed as a rich delicacy, to be eaten only in small quantities. His answer seemed to satisfy the officer. Afterwards we learned that the turkey was not a turkey at all but a vulture. The cook had set a snare and caught it in the camp.

Two chaplains, one Australian and one English, reached the camp about this time. Between them they built up the church, and, with it, the morale of many in the camp. At the same time a growing uneasiness gripped the Japanese. They ordered sudden roll-calls in the middle of the night, making us tumble out, then keeping us standing on parade, often well into the next day. They raided our huts without warning, seizing any books or papers they could discover.

In one of these raids I lost my diary, my Greek grammars and my Bible. I went to headquarters and demanded their return. The interpreter to whom I spoke surrendered my Bible, stamping his 'chop', or identifying mark, on the flyleaf. But he refused to give back my diary and laboriously compiled texts.

The Australian chaplain, Padre Hugh Cunningham, did not fare so well. The Japanese surprised him in the act of thumbing through a school atlas. For two days they confined him in a bamboo cell so low that he could not stand up in it, and so narrow that he could not sit down. To make doubly certain of his discomfort, a guard came by at intervals and prodded him with his bayonet.

Abruptly, our captors issued an order forbidding religious services, of which they had become increasingly suspicious. They had sworn to bring us to complete subjection; they had not done so. We were bent but not broken. Out of a condition of no purpose had appeared men with purpose. If this improvement continued, the guards reasoned, our gatherings could become a potential focus for revolt. They also reinforced the ban against singing, which they had relaxed after completion of the bridge.

We had no intention of complying. On information passed from mouth to mouth, small knots of men assembled in different parts of the camp at irregular intervals. Services were conducted somewhat in the manner of a Quaker meeting, with a lesson followed by questions and comment in the place of a formal sermon.

After a time, in response to our petition, the authorities

permitted us to resume our services. They stipulated, however, that a Japanese interpreter be present to make sure no one preached subversion.

Good Friday came, and most of us, regardless of denomination, decided to attend at noon the Roman Catholic service of the Stations of the Cross. We wanted to bow our heads and bend our knees before the Lord who had died for all of us.

In my contemplation I recognized that it was no easy thing to call that figure on the Cross 'Lord'. I heard again His words, 'Father, forgive them, for they know not what they do'. This He had said for His enemies; but what was I to say for mine? I could not say what He had said, for He was innocent, whereas I was not. Humbly, I had to ask, 'Forgive me *and* my enemies, for we know not what we do.'

I said to myself, 'By His death He gave to men the responsibility of caring for one another and doing His Father's will; to sons and mothers and fathers and sisters and brothers He assigned the task of caring for all other sons and mothers and fathers and sisters and brothers. No small commission.

'To call Him "Lord" meant there was no other way but His. Yet how could I follow Him? I knew the Sermon on the Mount, but I lived by the laws and conventions of society — a society that condemned criminals to isolation or death, whereas He led them to Paradise. I called Him "Lord", but with my fellow men worshipped Mammon in our temples of business. I had read that He was the Way, the Truth and the Life. But we still clung to the belief that man was master of his fate, capable of building the equivalent of God's Kingdom through his own knowledge, his skills and his technology.

'He asked us to believe in Him. But it was much easier for us to believe in a president or a dictator, a scientist, scholar, news commentator, cinema actress or football player. Any of these was more acceptable than a Jewish carpenter, condemned as a criminal, hanging on a bloody Cross.'

I confessed, 'It is hard to be a disciple, Lord.'

At dawn on Easter Sunday some of us slipped out of our huts to make our communion in the open at the edge of the camp. There we received the elements in token of our Lord's sacrifice, that we might be strengthened to follow 'the Comrade-God who on the cross was slain, to rise again'.

When we finished the sun was up. To the east, there were shadows; to the west, light.

10

THE LAST TREK

Again we received orders to move. We were to be separated from the other ranks and confined to a camp for officers only. Why, after three years, did the Japanese want to make such a change? The signs of uneasiness amongst them increased; there was something in the wind.

I learned that we were heading back to Kanburi, about sixty miles to the west of our present location. This was familiar territory. Near Kanburi had been the marshalling base for supplies to build the original bridge over the River Kwai; it was at this spot that I had boarded the barge which took us the few miles upriver to Chungkai. I wondered what Chungkai was like today. Did any prisoners still remain? Had the jungle reclaimed its own?

As the train clacked along its jungle track old memories stirred. In perspective, I could see that what I had experienced had been extraordinary – both at Chungkai and later at Nakawm Paton.

At first both had been places dominated by sickness and despair. Yet I had seen a Power at work to renew many of us. Men were still men, so I had seen selfishness. But I had also seen love. This love and the church without walls were related. The church, with all its imperfections, was the only visible earnest or guarantee of something greater. It set our feet on the way of an eternal pilgrimage and pointed us towards an unchanging goal – to the source of life and the City of God.

I recalled what Dostoevski had said in *The Possessed*:

> The one essential condition of human existence is that man should always be able to bow down before something infinitely great. If men are deprived of the infinitely great they will not go on living and die of despair. The Infinite and the Eternal are as essential for man as the little planet on which he dwells.

We had been at Kanburi only a few days when a guard informed us gleefully that Franklin D. Roosevelt was dead and that Winston Churchill was seriously ill and not expected to live. The Allied war effort was thus doomed to failure, and an Axis victory was imminent.

To counter this propaganda we had the evidence of our senses. The sight of Allied bombers overhead was no longer a rare occurrence. They appeared in the sky every day, scorning the chatter of the ack-ack battery mounted near the bridge. One morning the sirens sounded. This time the planes came in low and pattern-bombed the bridge. At the edge of our camp a train was standing. From the air the train made the area appear to be a legitimate military target. The fliers then pattern-bombed Kanburi, killing about forty men. The rest of us crouched in hastily made slit-trenches.

The bombing continued for several days. Although damaged slightly, the bridge was not destroyed. About a week later a rumble of thunder announced the approach of another raid. At the sound of the motors our guards dived for the nearest place of shelter. The squadron was well organized and thoroughly efficient in its task of destruction. As it zoomed overhead, two bombers detached themselves and swooped down on the ack-ack battery, silencing it in their first run. Then the formation broke up. Each plane, one at a time, made a run over the bridge. Against the blue skies the bombers were a pleasing picture as they circled to await their turns.

A plane passed and dropped its stick of bombs. A span of the bridge disappeared. Another plane and another dropped their loads. This went on until every span was smashed. Each time bombs hit a span, a cheer went up from the crowd of emaciated men, despite their own danger from the bombs.

None of us had any love for that bridge. I had become a hated symbol – a symbol of Japanese power and ruthlessness. Prisoners of war had been driven to build it against their will. And as officers we had been forced to take part.

We watched the heavy beams as they floated downstream from the site of the bridge to us at Kanburi. Many remembered how they had waded in with those timbers on their shoulders, fighting to keep from being swept away by the furious current. They remembered the makeshift piledriver and the impossible demands it made on their exhausted bodies as they lifted and dropped, lifted and dropped, its heavy weight.

They remembered their determined attempts at sabotage; the sawing of the bolts half through when the attention of the guards could be diverted; the unscrewing of nuts that had been passed as 'OK' and the smashing of their threads. They remembered one prisoner with an inventive turn of mind, who had gathered queens of the white ant, a large jungle termite, and buried them beside the timbers in the hope that they would eat away the supports.

The last span floated past. A belly-based cheer went up from Kanburi.

'Hey!' a voice beside me cried. 'What if the Nips make us build it all over again?'

'Don't worry,' said another consolingly, 'they haven't the heart for it.'

I could only hope he was right.

Nothing remained now of the bridge over the River Kwai

but a mass of wreckage, already far downstream. The bombers came over again to take a last admiring look at their handiwork. The sound of the engines died away into quiet, but not for long. Our guards, having crawled out of their hiding-places, reacted from fear with shouts and curses and threats.

No other such incidents occurred to break the monotony. But the work load was not heavy, and life might have been supportable except for the sadistic character of the camp commandant, who rightly belonged in a mental institution. He was a snarling misanthrope, a scowling, vicious sadist, ever on the look-out for trouble. He hated us, although we never knew why. He went out of his way to create situations he could use as an excuse to torment us. He regularly baited prospective victims into making statements which he could interpret as a reflection on the Emperor.

On one occasion a British interpreter went to the assistance of an officer who was being tortured, and recklessly protected him with his own body. Guards held the interpreter while the crazed commandant beat him with a heavy ruler. Still alive and bleeding profusely, the offender was thrown into a slit-trench. The commandant ordered him to be kept there. Only his strong will enabled him to survive until his release.

It was hard to love such a man as the commandant.

The tension in the camp increased. At almost any time of day or night the Japanese continued to spring their surprise raids. They kept us standing on parade while they searched our sleeping-places. But now we had so little that there wasn't much they could find. Many items, nevertheless, remained safely hidden; compasses, maps and knives. One officer even had a dachshund which he had kept with him all the way from Singapore.

The behaviour of our guards puzzled us. Were they planning to massacre us? We had to face that possibility. If so, I decided to make a bid for freedom – even if it turned out to be no more than a bid. I undertook a rigorous toughening-up programme. I was feeling better, apart from my periodic attacks of malaria, than at any time since my imprisonment. Every morning before reveille a friend and I did our exercises. We also volunteered to join a team operating the hand pump that gave the Japanese their water supply. This was hard work, but hard work was what we wanted.

Orders were then given for the whole camp to be moved, a few men at a time, to a new area north-east of Bangkok. Weary of Kanburi and its sour smells, I put in for one of the first parties to leave. Each consisted of about two hundred officers divided into three companies. One of my responsibilities as section commander was the distribution of equipment that had been allotted to us to carry, consisting of large, heavy dishes of awkward size, shovels, picks and hammers.

The spiritual growth which I had been witnessing for the past year or so had been mostly manifest among the other ranks. I had seen that attitude so well described by Lt-Gen. A. E. Percival in a letter written after the war:

> Every Sunday the Churches were filled, and where there were no churches and no chaplain, services were held in ordinary buildings or in the open air, and were conducted by the prisoners themselves. Inspired by faith, the British soldiers in these camps displayed some of the finest qualities of their race. Courageous under repression and starvation, patient through the long years of waiting, cheerful and dignified in the face of adversity, they steadfastly resisted all efforts of the Japanese to break their spirit and finally conquered.

I had been impressed by those same qualities. I had faith in our Jocks. I had watched their developing concern for one another. But, not having had the same experience with my brother officers, I wasn't so sure about them. Had the love of God touched them as well?

My doubts were soon dispelled. I was surprised to see how eagerly they accepted assignments and wanted to do what was best for the group as a whole. In fact, one band of officers came to me and offered to perform any especially unpleasant chores.

Eastward we travelled through Banpong towards Bangkok. All along the track we could see the damage done by the Allied air forces. Railway junctions and marshalling yards were in ruins. Often the train was switched to a temporary track, bypassing sections that had been wiped out. Occasionally we would wait while a train passed loaded with reinforcements bound for Burma. The troops looked woefully young. We even saw a cavalry regiment ride along the road. It had come all the way from China. Goodness knows how many months it had taken them to get this far. The ponies were scrawny; the leather in the reins and saddles was patched and broken.

Further on, we were shunted on to a siding for a lengthy stay. We found ourselves on the same track with several carloads of Japanese wounded. They were on their own and without medical care. No longer fit for action, they had been packed into railway trucks which were being returned to Bangkok. Whenever one of them died en route, he was thrown off into the jungle. The ones who survived to reach Bangkok would presumably receive some form of medical treatment there. But they were given none on the way.

They were in a shocking state; I have never seen men filthier. Their uniforms were encrusted with mud, blood and excrement. Their wounds, sorely inflamed and full of pus, crawled with maggots. The maggots, however, in eating the putrefying flesh, probably prevented gangrene.

We could understand now why the Japanese were so cruel to

their prisoners. If they didn't care a tinker's damn for their own, why should they care for us?

The wounded men looked at us forlornly as they sat with their heads resting against the carriages waiting fatalistically for death. They were the refuse of war; there was nowhere to go and no one to care for them. These were the enemy, more cowed and defeated than we had ever been.

Without a word, most of the officers in my section un-buckled their packs, took out part of their ration and a rag or two, and, with water canteens in their hands went over to the Japanese train to help them. Our guards tried to prevent us, bawling, 'No goodka! No goodka!' But we ignored them and knelt by the side of the enemy to give them food and water, to clean and bind up their wounds, to smile and say a kind word. Grateful cries of '*Aragatto*!' ('Thank you!') followed us when we left.

An Allied officer from another section of the train had been taking it all in. 'What bloody fools you all are!' he said to me. 'Don't you realize that those are the enemy?'

'Have you never heard the story of the man who was going from Jerusalem to Jericho?' I asked him. He gave me a blank look, so I continued, 'He was attacked by thugs, stripped of everything and left to die. Along came a priest; he passed him by. Then came a lawyer, a man of high principles; he passed by as well. Next came a Samaritan, a half-caste, a heretic, an enemy. But he didn't pass by; he stopped. His heart was filled with compassion. Kneeling down, he poured some wine through the unconscious lips, cleaned and dressed the helpless man's wounds, then took him to an inn where he had him cared for at his own expense.'

'But that's different!' the officer protested angrily. 'That's in the Bible. These are the swine who've starved us and beaten us. They've murdered our comrades. These are our enemies.'

'Who is mine enemy? Isn't he my neighbour? God makes

neighbours; we make enemies. You know full well that is where we excel. Mine enemy may be anyone who threatens my privileges – or my security – or my person – as well as those poor wretches who know no better. If they don't we, at least, should. Whether we like it or not, we are the ones who create the enemy and lose the neighbour. Mine enemy *is* my neighbour!'

He gave me a scornful glance and, turning his back, left me to my thoughts.

I regarded my comrades with wonder. Eighteen months ago they would have joined readily in the destruction of our captors had they fallen into their hands. Now these same men were dressing the enemy's wounds. We had experienced a moment of grace, there in those blood-stained railway cars. God had broken through the barriers of our prejudice and had given us the will to obey His command, 'Thou shalt love'.

The words of Jesus came to me: 'Ye have heard that it hath been said, Thou shalt love thy neighbour, and hate thine enemy. But I say unto you, love your enemies, bless them that curse you, do good to them that hate you, and pray for them which despitefully use you and persecute you; that ye may be the children of your Father who is in heaven.'

The reply Reason made to such a command was, 'But we have to be practical because we live in a practical world. It doesn't pay to love – particularly your enemy.'

Now Faith answered, 'Quite true. One need but to look at the Cross to see this demonstrated. But – there is no other way to love. "Except a grain of wheat fall into the earth and die, it abideth by itself alone."'

Our experience of life in death had taught us that the way to life leads through death. To see Jesus was to see in Him that love which is the very highest form of life, that love which has sacrifice as the logical end of its action. To hang on to life, to guard it jealously, to preserve it, is to end up by burying it. Each of us must die to the physical life of selfishness, the life controlled by our hates, fears, lusts and prejudices in order to live in the flesh the life that is of the spirit. This is a basic law that cannot be broken except at great cost.

We were beginning to understand that as there were no easy ways for God, so there were no easy ways for us. God, we saw, was honouring us by allowing us to share in His labours, aye, in His agony – for the world He loves. God, in finding us, had enabled us to find our brother.

A whistle blew. A train with a light load came along, picked up our cars and we were on our way. We found the bridge over the River Tachin had been knocked out – not so thoroughly as the one over the Kwai, but thoroughly enough. Juggling our kit and tools, we shuffled across on a single plank high above the water.

Once on the other side, several of us were conscripted to load barges ferrying supplies across the river. It was hard coolie work performed under acute pressure and in scorching heat. I tried to take a drink of water, but it made me froth at the mouth. A work-mate gave me a pinch of salt and I was myself again. The urgency with which the Japanese drove us had its cheering aspect – it could only mean that they were suffering reverses in Burma.

In Bangkok we were to be transferred from one railway station to another. We were marched along a picturesque canal, where a highly decorated barge made a graceful picture as it cut through the reflection of the gilded Wat Arun pagoda. Friendly Thais in their white suits and bright sarongs lined our path, shouting and cheering as we went by, obviously trying to tell us something. They held up their fingers in a V-for-Victory sign. We were familiar with the V-sign, but we had no idea what they were attempting to convey by it now. Did it express no more than partisan enthusiasm? Or did they have hopeful information? Mystified, but appreciating their gesture, I returned the salute.

Suddenly the smiling faces disappeared in a blaze of blackness. The next thing I knew I was lying on the ground, looking up at a guard standing over me ready to strike another blow. The indignant exclamations from the crowd, however, had their effect. After he had stormed at me for a while he lowered his rifle and allowed me to stagger to my feet. I considered the blow a fair price to pay for the friendship of the crowd.

When we reached the other station we were told that there would be an all-day wait for the train. Some POWs were working in the yard. I recognized two of them as Argylls. Jumping up quickly, I ran to meet them. But I was stopped short by a guard. Communication between different groups of prisoners was not tolerated.

I sat down in the shade of a warehouse close to the gang working under the watchful eye of a supervisor. Gradually I inched my way along without rising from a sitting position. After about an hour I reached the corner opposite the men. I gave a quick, low whistle. One of the Argylls glanced up, looked around, and was about to resume his work when he saw me sitting in the shadows.

'Come over towards me,' I called in a loud whisper, 'and we'll have a wee chat.'

He nodded to show that he had heard me. Then, keeping his back towards me, he pushed his hand-truck in my direction. He threw a box on the ground. As he stooped to pick it up, he said, 'We'll have to be awfully careful. The Nips are keeping a tight guard on us.'

'That's not a bad sign,' I replied. 'It must mean they've got the wind up. Do you have any news?'

He threw another box on the ground.

'Not even a rumour. We're a small camp – run by a Nip

warrant officer. He's a regular bastard. We're always being beaten up and having our rations cut.'

'Cheer up,' I said. 'We passed through Bangkok a while ago. The Thais look happy about something. I'm sure the news must be good. By the way, could you use any money?'

'Could I? Me and two other Argylls are mucking in together. One of them is pretty sick. The rest of us try to keep him going. If I could buy some food — '

'How can you buy food if the Nips won't let you speak to the Thais?'

'Nothing to it. We bribe the guards.'

He glanced over his shoulder. 'The Pig has his eye on me. I'd better finish this load.'

The guard was coming in his direction. He moved the hand-cart nearer the truck and lifted his last box. Picking up the handle of the empty cart, he passed near enough to whisper, 'I'll be back.'

The Pig was now quite close and stood berating him. He was facing the sun so he couldn't see me in the shadows. I sat there without moving, waiting for the Argyll to come back. After a long ten minutes he returned, pulling an enormous stack of boxes.

'You'd think I was a bloody donkey, wouldn't you?' He brought the cart to a stop. Then he said, 'You'd better hop it or they'll beat the life out of you.'

'Dinna worry,' I replied, 'they'll not do that.' I fumbled at my waist, where I had over fifty bahts of my pay tucked. 'I'm putting this money under a stone. When you've finished, pick it up.'

I held up the stone for him to see; then I placed it on top of the bahts.

'Best of luck. Give my love to the boys.'

'That I'll do. And thanks for the cash.'

'Goodbye, Jock. God bless you.'

'Goodbye, sir. And God bless you.'

Under the watchful eye of the Pig, he resumed loading more energetically than before, while I inched my way back along the shadows to rejoin my party.

It was well after dark when our train came. We rode all night standing up, and at dawn were dumped by a roadside and ordered to march. We found ourselves in the midst of paddy fields stretching away into nowhere. We began to march. As the sun climbed, the heat became stifling, for it was about the hottest part of the year. At noon we were halted briefly and allowed to boil some water to drink. There was nothing left to eat, as our journey had taken longer than expected.

As we took the road again, a big car drove up. A Japanese officer glared at us, glanced at his watch, told our guards to hurry us up, then drove away. The heat grew so intense that the metal of our tools and utensils blistered our fingers at the touch. Again we had no water or salt. The afternoon seemed unending.

With the coming of night the temperature dropped and it seemed chilly by contrast. Then the skies opened and it began to rain with sudden tropical ferocity. The road was a quagmire and the whole countryside was a swamp. Our packs took on the weight of lead. At every step the suction of the mud dragged us down. Some faltered and could not go on. Their burdens were shouldered by others. With our arms around the flagging ones, we made it into Camp Nakon Nyok at about four in the morning. It had taken us almost twenty-four hours to march the forty miles.

We were assigned space in a half-completed hut and fell asleep as we were, drenched and caked with mud. At six I was awakened with a shake and ordered to produce four officers at once for a work party. I thought this was barbarous and said so at once. But no one paid attention.

Taking note of our surroundings, we found that we were

right in the middle of a military position the Japanese were preparing for their defence. It was apparently intended to block an invasion following a possible Allied landing on the coast near Bangkok. We were at the base of the foothills. Between us and the shore there was nothing but a great flat plain of paddy fields. Troops came and went. We could hear big guns being moved into place. On a steep hill above us we could see an observation post being constructed. Here the Japanese were apparently making ready for a last desperate stand.

We had to admit that our prospects did not look bright. Japanese officers scowled at us as they rode by on horseback. The air crackled with tension. The camp commandant, the same one we'd had at Kanburi, appeared and was immediately more demanding and nastier than ever. Every day there was a cluster of prisoners staked to the ground in front of the guard house. We had no news of the war's progress, but we could feel that something important was in the wind.

One morning we had gone to work as usual. This time we were to carry rocks down the hill to ballast the road we were building. About mid-morning our guards disappeared. We took advantage of their absence by lying down to rest. After several hours they returned drunk. They motioned us to pack up and go back to the camp.

'This is it!' I said excitedly to Blondie, a friend of mine, as we started back to camp.

'What do you mean?'

'The Japs are licked. The show is over. They've thrown in the sponge.'

Blondie was more conservative. 'Take it easy, don't get your hopes up,' he said. 'Tell me what you've got to go on.'

We were marching past the guard house. The ground in front of it was empty.

'What do you make of that, Blondie? Where do you suppose the poor blighters are who were staked out there this morning?'

He refused to be impressed.

'Oh, I dunno. Perhaps they've been released.'

'You can bet they've been released. Tell me – when do you remember seeing that piece of ground free of prisoners? And they're not the only ones who'll be released. Wait and see.'

'Oh, I dunno,' he said. 'I dunno about that.'

About the middle of the evening, news spread through the tense, expectant huts that the Japanese commandant had sent for Lt Colonel Toosey, the British senior officer. I was sitting in our hut with John Leckie and several other old friends, wondering what was happening. We hadn't long to wait for an answer. Word flashed from one end of the camp to the other. In the dim light of the palm-oil lamp faces shone. Silently we shook hands.

Someone started singing. Then everyone was singing with all his power. The song was quickly taken up; it resounded from hut to hut. From everywhere it came – the words of Elgar's 'Pomp and Circumstance':

> *Land of hope and glory,*
> *Mother of the free,*
> *How shall we extol thee,*
> *Who are born of thee?*
>
> *Wider still and wider*
> *Shall thy bounds be set;*
> *God who made thee mighty,*
> *Make thee mightier yet!*

Next we sang 'God Save the King', 'Jerusalem the Golden' and the 23rd Psalm. We sang and we kept on singing. It was hearty singing – the singing of free men.

We noticed that our guards had all melted into the night. There was a reason for this. The Japanese military had been accustomed to singing war-chants to nerve themselves for battle. When they heard our hearty singing they concluded that we were preparing to slaughter them, so they took to the hills.

It was late before the camp was allowed to return to silence.

Before reveille I was outside the hut, doing my exercises, when I sensed that I was being watched. Turning round, I saw a guard standing at attention about ten yards away. When he caught my eye he bowed and kept on bowing. I thought at first he must be trying to imitate me. But his bows weren't deep enough for that.

Not knowing what else to do, I smiled at him. He smiled back.

'*Okayga?*'

'*Okayga.*'

Without waiting for further word, he streaked for the hills. Presumably he had been chosen to find out what we planned to do. The Japanese soon afterwards returned to their quarters, one or two at a time, keeping their distance. Though we now held the power, it never occurred to us to raise a hand against them.

The moment of grace by the railway siding was no temporary experience. The same situation held true in other camps. The liberators were so infuriated by what they saw that they wanted to shoot the Japanese on the spot. Only the intervention of the victims prevented them. Captors were spared by their captives. 'Let mercy take the place of bloodshed,' said these exhausted but forgiving men. 'Not an eye for an eye, a limb for a limb.'

Like faith and forgiveness, freedom isn't something just to be talked about. It has to be enacted. After breakfast, John Leckie and I felt that on this our first morning of freedom we had to climb the hill behind the camp. While we made our way to the top, we saw that others had had the same impulse. There were scattered groups of men, some ahead of us, some behind us, going up in silence. We reached the top. Stretching out before us, as far as we could see, was the brown-and-green patchwork quilt of the paddy fields. We stood in quiet reverence, gazing out over those fields to the horizon, towards Chungkai, where our friends had died, and we spoke the words of Psalm 121, 'I will lift up mine eyes unto the hills.'

Freedom burst out all over. When the Japanese commandant had read the order granting POWs permission to fly their flags and to play national anthems they were only carrying out a formality. They did not expect these things to happen. At a nearby camp, however, within minutes of the reading of the order, an enormous Union Jack was fluttering bravely from the flagpole. That banner had been carried through the death camps of the railway for that very moment by an Argyll who never doubted that the day of victory would come. The Japanese had not found it, for he had made his blanket into a sleeping-bag with the Union Jack lining it.

At our own camp a flag was quickly found and hoisted. As we looked at it waving proudly, we saw it as a symbol of our liberty – our liberty founded on the Cross; for the Union Jack is composed of three crosses, the Cross of St George, the Cross of St Patrick and the Cross of St Andrew.

Soon afterwards, a fellow Argyll, David Boyle, had the pleasure of going to the Japanese commandant and demanding a battery to operate our wireless. The commandant stared at him. 'Battery? Wireless? But you can't have a wireless!'

'We've had one here for quite a while,' David informed him.

'But how? How did you get it in?'

'*You* brought it in for us.'

'No. I wouldn't do that.'

'You did, though. You brought it in from Kanburi – with that loot you had in your baggage.'

The commandant was speechless. David went on, 'We knew your searches were so thorough that we hadn't a chance in hell

of smuggling the wireless into camp unless we sent it in with
you.'

'But . . . but . . . ' The commandant was still nonplussed.

David spelled it out for him. 'Remember the squad you
detailed to load your baggage for you? They slipped the set
in . . . Another squad slipped it out again after you got
here . . . Now, how about that battery?'

'Certainly, certainly,' said the commandant, coming to attention and bowing. 'You shall have it right away.'

'Quite,' David said crisply. He turned his back on the commandant and walked out. The list of this officer's crimes was
so long that he was sentenced by his own superiors to life
imprisonment. Soon after that he was tried again by the Allied
tribunal and received the death sentence.

We put our wireless into operation at once. We learned then
that Russia had declared war on Japan, and that the atom
bombs had been dropped. But we also learned of the Japanese
directive ordering that if Admiral Mountbatten landed troops
in Thailand all officers in prison camps were to be killed. At
the same time we learned that our new camp had been observed and was presumed to be a location for Japanese
troops. Therefore it was scheduled to be bombed by the RAF.
The Mountbatten landings were set for 28 August, the RAF
bombings for 17 August. Since the day of liberation was 16
August, we had a very narrow margin of safety. Had the war
continued for two more weeks, we would have copped it one
way or another, at the hands of friend or foe.

We stayed on in camp to await orders. The Japanese quarter
masters released Red Cross parcels to us. Our faces fell when
we saw that they were marked 'September 1942'. We found
their contents completely unusable.

Whatever entertainment there might be we had to provide
for ourselves, but we were old hands at it by now. Willing
workers quickly erected a stage on which was produced a

Liberty Revue, including a Victory Can-Can danced and sung by a chorus of 'the short and the fat and the tall'. Ponies were confiscated from a Japanese cavalry unit for a genuine Liberty Derby.

Our first visitor from the outside world was an American paratrooper who had lost his way and wandered into our camp. We wondered what he must have thought as he was seized by a yelling crowd of skinny, bronzed, bearded, half-naked savages who bore him on their shoulders through the camp. For hours we bombarded him with questions, while he recounted, step by step, the entire course of the war, regaling us with everything that had happened during our three-and-a-half years of silence. To us he was the living embodiment of the freedom we had longed for all that time.

11

THROUGH THE VALLEY

Communications of a sort were soon established. Ox-carts bumped along the muddy roads, bringing medicines, and decent clothing and eventually mail. This time I was among the lucky ones. When the G's were called there was a packet of blue envelopes addressed in my father's bold handwriting – just as I had seen them in my dreams many months before. For the first time in four years I learned of what had been happening at home.

But there was something we craved even more than mail – news of our missing comrades – especially news of those who had gone up-country on some work party and had not been heard of again. Were they still alive? How had they fared? The men in the ration parties made it their business to gather all the information they could and pass it on from one camp to the next. The minute they entered camp eager prisoners would surround them and pelt them with questions.

'Have ye heard anything of my mucker? Name of McIntosh. He was a sergeant in the Field Artillery – the 122nd. About middle-sized, he was. With dark-brown hair. Expect he'd be wearing a beard.'

Usually the couriers shook their heads. Occasionally a name would give them a clue. Now and then the news was good; more often it was not. Death was continuing to take its toll. The name uppermost for me was Dusty Miller's. Whenever an ox-cart appeared I was in the front rank of questioners. I was looking forward to a reunion with Dusty and Dinty Moore. At every opportunity I asked visitors from other camps if they had any word. Time and again I put the same question and gave the descriptions. Repeatedly I received the same reply, 'Sorry chum, I don't remember anyone by that name – or of that description. Could you give me a clue?'

It was from one of the couriers that I learned how Dinty Moore had died. But there was still no word of Dusty. Then at last I met a prisoner who had been on the same work detail with him. 'Yes, I knew him,' he said. 'We were sent to Burma to cut a retreat route for the Japs. He was one of those left behind after the road was built to maintain it during the monsoon.'

'Where is he now?' I asked.

The man was reluctant to speak. He stammered for a minute or two. Then he replied, 'We had a pretty bad time of it. It was a repeat performance of the railway. And those who were left behind had an even harder time – especially after the Japs heard that defeat was possible.'

He stopped.

'But what about Miller?' I asked again.

The man looked away.

'The last news I had of him wasn't good.'

'What was it, then?'

'According to what I heard, he was in trouble.'

'Dusty?'

'He got the Nip warrant officer in charge of his party down on him.'

'What had he done wrong?'

'That was it. He hadn't done anything wrong.' He swallowed hard. 'The Nip hated him because he couldn't break him. You know how he was – a good man if ever there was one. That's why he hated him.'

'What did the Nip do to him?'

'He strung him up to a tree.'

I was aghast. 'You mean . . .'

Then came the simple reply. 'Yes. He crucified him.'

I could hardly speak.

'When?'

'About the beginning of August.'

'Just before the Japs . . .'

' . . . packed up, yes.'

He turned away. He had said as much as he could bear to. I was so stunned that I didn't quite know what to do. I walked out from the group of chattering questioners in a daze.

Dusty dead? Dusty – the man of deep faith and warm heart – the man who was incapable of a mean act, even against a brutal tormentor. His goodness, it is true, had been recognized, not in sympathy, however, but in hate. Condemned by such radiant goodness, the warrant officer must have gone berserk.

There on that tree, like his Master, he died, so far from his homeland, so far from everyone, yet so near to God.

I moved off to a corner of the camp that I might bear my grief alone. Tears clouded my eyes. The surroundings misted so that nothing was clear any more; there was only the reality of suffering, disappointment and sorrow.

As I sat with my back resting against the prison fence, I could see once again the light that had challenged the darkness in the valley of the shadow – light that had been reflected from gentle faces. I could see Dusty kneeling before me, a rag in his hand, a basin in front of him, as he cleaned my ulcers, his smiling face uplifted. I could see Dinty Moore donating the gift of his quick wit and kindly humour as he performed some menial task. I could see Dodger Green as he talked eagerly and wistfully, enquiring about the truth he was beginning to apprehend. I could see Ian Carruthers remembering the days of his boyhood and the yachts that sailed the Clyde. I could see the young lad holding my hand and asking, 'It's all right, isn't it, sir?'

The words of St Paul came to me, 'For God, who comman-
deth the light to shine out of the darkness, hath shined in our
hearts, to give the light of knowledge of God in the face of
Jesus Christ.'

I could see so many faces shining with God's light. It was
that light which had helped me to see in my own darkness.

When we thought of returning home we saw ourselves as
ghosts of the past. The Britain most of us had known was the
Britain of 1939. Six years had gone by; and six years is a long
time when one is in one's twenties. Our families and friends
would have changed as well as we. They had known us as
boys; we were going back as war-hardened men.

On a night of hammering rain the order came, 'Pack up!
You're on your way to Bangkok!' We began the last lap out as
we had ended the last lap in, slogging it on foot through that
heavy, squelchy mud. But this time trucks were waiting for us
at the road end – trucks with respectful Japanese at the wheel.
On our way across Bangkok to the airfield we passed by the
spot where the guard had struck me with his gun butt for
holding up my fingers in the V-sign. It had happened only a
short while ago, yet the event seemed of another age.

While we waited in the hangar for our plane to come, we
saw our first white woman in three and a half years, a blonde,
shapely Norwegian. She had been interned with her husband,
and had come to feed the former POWs. She was beautiful.
The sight of her reminded us that there were other places and
other ways of living and that we were on our way back to
them.

The Japanese had given us the backlog of pay due to us for
three and a half years. It was in bahts, which had dropped so
greatly in value that when four of us who were travelling
together pooled our resources we had barely enough to buy a
fruit salad. We argued over the amount of vitamins in that

salad, but agreed that it was far tastier than the vitamin pills we were now being given in huge quantities to swallow daily.

Next morning our group boarded a Dakota en route for Rangoon. Our pilot, having heard that I had been a flyer at one time, kindly invited me to join him as co-pilot. He was watching me as I followed closely the trail of the railway etched across the valley of the Kwai.

'I'll bet you're glad to be away from all that,' he said.

'Yes,' I replied. 'That I am.'

'We heard from time to time how you were being treated,' he said. 'Native agents smuggled word through to Intelligence. It must have been tough, all right.'

We were flying up the valley along our railway, past the empty place where the bridge had been across the River Kwai, past Chungkai, Touchan, Kinao, Takanun, places we had known so well – places that were the graveyards of so many of our friends. Our trip, which otherwise was like a holiday outing, was saddened by these memories.

We had not only come through the valley, we were above it. We were on the high road home – a road that had taken me six years to find. I recalled the words of the old Scots song:

> *For ye'll tak' the high road and I'll tak' the low road,*
> *And I'll be in Scotland afore ye;*
> *For me and my true love will never meet again*
> *On the bonnie, bonnie banks of Loch Lomond.*

According to what I had been told as a child, this was a message sent by a Highland chief to his beloved before his execution in Carlisle during Prince Charlie's retreat from the attainment of his hopes and of his kingdom. The low road was the way of death – the way so many of my comrades had taken.

A poignant recollection stirred in my mind. I had been

wounded in the right shoulder in Malaya, and sent back to Singapore to recover. Before I was released to rejoin the remnant of the battalion I learned that my friend Gordon Shiach had been badly hurt and was in another hospital. I had known Gordon when we were schoolboys, and we had been together on a cruise for Scottish secondary schools in the Baltic. I hadn't seen him again until the day I left Stirling Castle as he was entering with a squad of recent recruits. Eventually he had been posted to us in Singapore.

When the battalion was in action in Malaya he had been returning from brigade headquarters with a supply of maps when he was attacked by an enemy tank. Although desperately wounded in the stomach, he had continued to drive his wreck of a car back to the battalion. As soon as I saw him, I knew that the end was not far off. His brown eyes stared at me as I entered his room. He recognized me, smiled as I greeted him, and said, 'I'm glad to see you. You're a breath of home.'

It would have been pointless to bring him any delicacies since he could eat nothing, so I had brought him a little book containing excerpts of prose and poetry about Scotland. I gave it to him and said, 'There, that'll give you a picture of what things are like.'

Thumbing through the book, he stopped at one place, and read.

'Yes, that's home all right.'

He looked up and handed me the book open at the 'Canadian Boat Song'. While I read I could see home through Gordon's eyes. There was the wide Firth stretching out before me as I stood on one of the Cowal hills that watched over it. On the silver-blue, ever-changing waters were the white wings of the yachts bearing their happy crews along on pleasant cruises. The Sleeping Warrior of Arran and the hills of the Atlantic coastline formed a velvet picture-frame for the homeland we knew so well:

Listen to me as when of old our father
Sang songs of other shores,
Listen to me and then in chorus gather
All your deep voices as you pull your oars.

Fair these broad meads, these hoary woods are grand,
But we are exiles from our native land.

From the lone shieling of the misty island
Mountains divide us, and the waste of seas—
Yet still the blood is strong, the heart is Highland,
As we in dreams behold the Hebrides.

A dark shadow stirred in the corner of the ward. The summer breeze of Scottish hills was displaced by the sticky heat of Singapore. Both of us felt the same sharp thrust of homesickness.

Like Gordon, all of us had our dream of home. We had fought for it on the battlefield; it had sustained many of us in the prison camp. But not all of these would ever see home again. Those of us who had survived were on our way back. Others would follow, flying above the River Kwai. This brought to mind the words of Isaiah: 'And an highway shall be there, and a way, and it shall be called the Way of Holiness; the unclean shall not pass over it; but it shall be for those: the wayfaring men, though fools, shall not err therein.'

We were far up along the river, nearing the Three Pagodas Pass. A storm struck us, and the pass was wreathed in a veil of swirling clouds and ghost-like shadows. Then for a moment the clouds parted. There was a burst of sunlight. Far below we could see the end of the valley.

It looked so small.

The clouds closed in again. We continued on our way.

EPILOGUE
...AND AFTER

The Dakota circled over Rangoon to give us our first view of the city and the first glimpse of our Army in occupation. Tree-fringed lakes and the Great Pagoda contributed to the air of peace and serenity. Immediately we landed we were escorted to a huge marquee staffed by members of the Women's Volunteer Service from Great Britain. The tent was filled with tables set for tea; smiling English ladies in light tropical dresses were in attendance. It is hard to describe the exquisite taste of the freshly-made white bread sandwiches and the freshly-brewed tea. We were able to taste and see things in a new way and to enjoy them so much more than we ever had before.

I was savouring my sixth cup when I looked up to see four men waiting near me as one of the ladies came to their table with tea. They had tears in their eyes and their Adam's apples were working overtime. These men were tough, tougher than most. They had proved that they could stand up to beatings and torture. But to be served with kindness had moved them so deeply that they sat silently, chokingly, in great humility. The Eternal Mercy had touched them and won them as the love of the Father had won the Prodigal on his return from the Far Country. There was a beauty about those four men as, barefoot and sun-blackened, they strove to hide their emotions.

We checked in at the military hospital set up in the

dormitories and buildings of Rangoon University by Lake Victoria. Our rags were taken from us and burned. We were given green jungle shirts and trousers, soap and towel, tooth-brush and tooth-paste. I watched my blanket being tossed on the fire. When they held it up I could see daylight through it. In the centre was a huge round patch of orange canvas which made it look like a darkened Japanese flag.

We could hardly eat. The tea had been more than sufficient for us, and our supper consisted of stew and canned peaches. It was to be a long time before I could eat meat again without feeling a stab of pain in the stomach. That night, as I tucked myself into a real bed with real sheets, I sighed in contentment.

Next morning, when one of the nursing sisters entered the ward, she said, 'I've never had patients like these in all my nursing experience. Every one has made his own bed, and men are competing for the privilege of sweeping the wards.' This expressed the attitude of these POWs. They lived not to be served but to serve.

At the end of October we embarked on a Dutch ship for Blighty. Our feelings were mixed as we waved farewell to Rangoon, the East and our years of captivity. The jungle had been challenging, there had been comradeship of the highest order, and we had found a way of life that proved to be vital, meaningful and beautifully sane. By the deaths of so many of our friends we were tied to those places with invisible cords that could never be broken.

I was musing by the rail when I noticed my friend John Leckie standing next to me. 'Well,' he said, 'it's all over. I wouldn't have missed it for anything. It was rough, all right. But I learned an awful lot that I couldn't have learned at the university or anywhere else. For one, I've learned about the real things of life, and, for another, it's great to be still alive.'

I knew exactly what had made him say this. The experiences we had passed through had deepened our understanding of life and of each other. We had looked into the heart of the Eternal and found Him to be wonderfully kind.

We made our first contact with the world we had left behind us as we were steaming up the Mersey to our berth in Liverpool. Word went around the ship that the dockers were on the point of striking for higher wages. They agreed, however, to handle our ship before they did so. Our Jocks were worried that people on shore might not get their rations if ships were not permitted to dock, and sent a delegation to see me about it. 'Couldn't we work the docks?' their spokesman asked. 'After all, we've done it before and we can do it again.'

I promised I'd do what I could. As soon as we landed I went to a harbour-master. He heard me out, all the time looking at me as if I were daft. Then he told me that to accept the Jocks' proposal would precipitate a national crisis. The labour unions would oppose it; the Army would forbid it. We thought we had come home to freedom. While we were prisoners we had been free to contribute to the general good, to help create order out of disorder. Here, in a society which paid lip service to freedom, we were prohibited, apparently, from applying the lessons we had learned. Impersonal laws, red tape, regulations in triplicate, were hemming us in like the jungle with invisible walls.

This harsh impression, however, was mellowed by the warm welcome from the friendly citizens who shouted, shook our hands and thrust bottles of beer upon us as our lorries drove through the streets of Liverpool.

An express train took us to Glasgow. My brother was waiting at the station barrier. I went with him to the hotel to cancel the reservation he had made in my name, as I had arrived in time to get home for the night. I thought I was looking fairly respectable in my battle-jacket and kilt, war-stained though it was. But the hall porter thought otherwise.

He told me that filthy luggage such as mine could not be left in the hall. I glanced down at my gear; to my eyes my mud-stained green army pack and kit-bag looked decent enough. I picked up the offending items to take them away before some civilian had his tender sensibilities affronted by a dab or two of mud and blood.

The day of the soldier was over.

A November moon shone brightly over the hills in the early morning hours, its face reflected on the surface of the Firth of Clyde, as I saw again the familiar shape of the home where I had said, 'Goodbye, Mother', 'Goodbye, Dad', six long years before. Lights burned in the windows. My parents were waiting up to welcome me. This meeting was the greatest shock of all. Time had not dealt kindly with them. The years of uncertainty and fears, of waiting, hoping and praying, had taken heavy toll. I had left them in summer; I had returned in winter.

Home again. But for what and to do what?

First we had to cope with the exasperating mechanics of re-adjustment, each experience bringing its own rude revelation. I was far luckier than most, for I was helped through my own readjustment by the sympathy of a girl who met me on my return, Helen McIntosh Robertson of Sandbank. I had known Helen for a long time, although we had had no matrimonial intentions. We renewed our friendship and after seventeen days she was brave enough to marry me.

The soldier-into-civilian troubles began almost as soon as we stepped off the train. On the day before I was to be demobbed I came down with one of my recurrent attacks of malaria. My teeth were chattering and I was shivering as I passed through the demobilization centre. I suggested that perhaps my discharge ought to be deferred until I had proper medical treatment. This put sand in the well-oiled machinery, and, in fact, caused it to stagger to a standstill. The medical officer told me firmly that nothing could be done. Once on the conveyor belt, I had to stay there until discharged at the other end in a 'civvy' suit.

When I grew stubborn about it someone pressed the panic button. A solemn-looking individual appeared and questioned me with the professional patience of one accustomed to dealing with difficult children or imbeciles. He finally asked me what I thought was wrong.

'Malaria!' I retorted, 'that's what's wrong!'

'M-hmm,' he said, as though disposing of that irrelevancy. Then, fixing me with a standard smile, he asked, 'Is there something worrying you, or are you afraid of anything?'

'Yes, I'm very much afraid that I'm going to have malaria at my own expense – whereas I would rather have it at the Army's.'

'Quite understandable – quite, quite,' he said, nodding sagely. Then, to humour me, he added, 'Now that you're home, you know, you've absolutely nothing to worry about – nothing at all, whatever.'

Conscious that I was up against an immovable object, I smiled as sweetly as I could, and enquired, 'How do you know?' Then I added abruptly, 'Never mind. I've had no medical treatment in the last three and a half years, I expect I can do without it now.'

I stepped back into line; the machine shuddered into action again, and I emerged with my grey flannel suit. It was too short and too wide.

A few weeks later I was admitted as a civilian to a hospital for tropical diseases, and was diagnosed as suffering not only from malaria but also from avitaminosis, hepatitis, enlarged heart, and ulcerated intestines from harbouring unfriendly amoebae. It took eight weeks to straighten me out, but I was to follow a restricted programme for the next two years. This included swigs of hydrochloric acid with every meal, for the acid buds of my stomach had been destroyed.

I was faced with a clothing problem; all I had to put on my back was the cheap, ill-fitting suit. When I went to the stores I learned no suits were available because of rationing. Then I was told with a sly wink that if I produced someone who could grant a favour for a favour, a transaction might be arranged. So much, it seemed, was done on this basis.

When it came to choosing our life's work we found many forces operating to frustrate our enthusiasms. We had been sent as boys to do men's work on the battlefield. Now that we returned as men we were offered boys' work. Counsellors with grey hair admonished us from behind their desks that we could now begin to live the British way by 'joining the team', 'toeing the line' and 'getting on the ball'. Concerning affairs of state, wiser heads than ours would guide us. The inference was that now we were out of prison camp we could put God away until Sunday. And with Him, our neighbour.

In some respects I could sympathize with this point of view. We weren't easy to live with; we were tense and taut and could not remain long doing nothing. Rather than sit in a chair we would pace the floor; rather than stay at home we would go out and walk for miles. Our sleeps were of short duration. As soon as we awoke we'd be on the prowl again, looking for something to do or someone to meet.

We had enormous reserves of nervous energy to be used. Ideas popped up in our mind with amazing rapidity. Convinced that every one was good, we would rush from place to place, trying to put them into action. Brazenly we told our political friends how the country should be governed; we told our friends in the school system what they ought to do to improve education; we told our friends in the clergy how to bring churches up to date.

It is not surprising that we were moody, restless and irritable.

We felt that at any moment we might be seized and deprived of our freedom. The Japanese were still with us; they entered our dreams. If we dreamed of the day's events in our new environment the guards would be there, walking unnoticed among the people in the street. If we strolled past with a friend they'd reach out and grab us. If we dreamed of open fields or rolling moors our old hosts would be there, advancing, closing in on us from every side. No matter how hard we tried to flee they would always catch us.

We hungered for one another's company and for the comradeship we shared. Our friends must have had the impression that our imprisonment was one huge, rollicking party. We fought off a great loneliness – a loneliness that was increased by the fact that so many of our friends had not returned. Old familiar spots were haunted with their faces.

Whenever we met with other former POWs we loved to talk of the brilliant plans we'd made and the great things we were going to do. We were convinced that we had learned lessons important to mankind and we were eager to implement them. We thought we had come home to a world at peace; instead we found a world already preparing for the next war. Having had as much reason to hate as anybody, we had overcome hatred. Yet we returned to a world divided by hatreds. Communist hated capitalist; capitalist hated communist; Arab hated Jew; Jew hated Arab; labour hated management; management hated labour; politician hated politician.

A moral cynicism was sapping the strength of society. Half-lies were not only condoned but regarded as smart. There were many who had remained untouched by the welter of the holocaust. What had happened on the battlefields, in mass bombings, in concentration camps – the blood, pain, suffering, heart-break and death – remained totally beyond their comprehension. They did not share in the hopes and agonies of mankind; they had no sense of involvement; they had no part in the universal fellowship of those who bear the mark of pain. Ever so brightly and ever so meanly they prostrated themselves before the Almighty Dollar and the Trembling Pound. We encountered some who were actually sorry to see the war end because they had such a good time and had done so well financially. Nations had survived this war, but few people asked, 'For what?'

The men with dry souls said, 'Let us go back to the good old days.' They wanted to draw the blinds on everything that had happened in between. There were no lessons to be learned, no decisions made, no risks taken, no new pilgrimages started, no adventures in partnership with God begun.

Everyone spoke of seeking security. But what did security mean but animal comfort, anaesthetized souls, closed minds and cold hearts? It meant a return to the cacophonous cocktail party as a substitute for fellowship, where, with glass in hand, men would touch each other but never meet. They would speak, but nothing would be said and nothing heard. They would look at their partners, but would not see them. With glassy eyes they would stare past them into nothingness.

It meant a return to the cheap love made possible by contraceptives, wherein male and female used each other as a thing, taking their share of sex in the same way as they took their cocktails and wondering where was the fulfilment, where was the satisfaction. With the despairing cry of 'I must be loved!' they would return periodically from the psychiatrist's couch to seek new partners and new problems. All the while their ears remained closed to the divine imperative, '*Thou shalt love!*'

It meant a return to the sedative at night and the stimulant in the morning; drugged sleep dulled the pain of existence and perked-up glands helped one face the fears of the day.

It meant a return to the faceless mass; to culture dragged down to the level of advertising media; to education, not as an instrument for enrichment and enlightenment of minds, but as a tool for mass conditioning. It meant a return to faith in technology and the Big Machine. As their powers were used to unleash yet greater hidden forces in Nature, so men could find themselves more enslaved than ever and ever readier to use those forces to bring about the total destruction of mankind. The contributions of free men seeking to serve the Infinitely Great in honesty, responsibility and love would be denied. Socrates would have to drink his cup of hemlock again, the prophets be stoned afresh. Atheistic materialism would fetter men to a hard, knobbly universe in which humanity was rejected.

In short, it meant flight from God and descent into the hell of loneliness and despair.

And where, in all this, was the vision of the Infinitely Great? Where was the place for those who wished to follow that vision, inspired, sustained and uplifted by it to find the way to serve their neighbour – and through serving their neighbour to serve their God, and so fulfil themselves? The vision of the Infinitely Great had been revealed to us by divine grace in the prison camp by the River Kwai. Now that we were back among the distractions and diversions of a materialistic world, we were determined to follow that vision. In my conversations with other former POWs I found many who were thinking as I was. With tremendous urgency, they were seeking vocations in which they could be of service to others.

As for myself, I thought at first I would return to the Far East, not, as I had envisioned on the *Setia Berganti*, to be Adviser-in-Chief to the Sultan of Somewhere, but to engage in social work or to teach in Japan. These prospects, however, did not work out. I then decided to follow the path along which I had been directed by my experiences in prison camps, and go to study theology in preparation for the ministry.

In many ways it was no easy choice to make, for it necessitated adjustment to an entirely different environment, language and attitude. After my return I had gone to church every

Sunday, but what I saw and heard depressed me. The sermons belonged to a different age. They suggested Victorian parlours, elderly people dressed in black, horsehair chairs and antimacassars. We had seen a vision of far horizons and caught a glimpse of the City of God in all its beauty, and this vision seemed to be part of a different world from that of the pulpit.

Yet I kept to my resolve and went for two years to theological college in Edinburgh. At the end of that time I received a fellowship at Hartford Theological Seminary in Connecticut. For two years I lived there with my wife, pursuing postgraduate studies in history. My choice was not unusual among former POWs. For years I kept hearing of former alumni of the hell camps who had gone into the ministry after having been in some other profession.

Among them was the Rev. Paul Miller, who is the vicar at Conor in Derbyshire. When he invited a Japanese from Hiroshima, the Rev. John Kanoh, to be his curate, his parishioners resented the appointment, remembering the fate that their brothers, sons and friends had suffered at the hands of the enemy. Mr Miller told his irate congregation, 'I want you to accept our newcomer as a member of the family.'

Later on he said to reporters, 'It was grim being a prisoner on the Burma railway, but I don't hold any bitterness for the Japanese. Their way of life is completely different. Japanese soldiers were severely punished by their own NCOs, so one would not expect them to treat prisoners with kindness.

'There are bound to be people in the village who won't like there being a Japanese curate. They will probably gossip about him in the pubs and clubs. I don't expect anyone to come directly to me and complain. The talking will be behind one's back. If any in the parish try to make things difficult for Father Kanoh, I shall visit them privately and give them a scolding – and it won't be mild.'

Many other POWs chose their calling with the objective of

serving their fellow man and contributing to the good of society. To this end they became teachers, welfare officers, research technicians or doctors. Among them was my friend John Leckie, who took up the study of medicine after he was demobbed. The last time I heard from him he was serving a coal-mining community in Wales, dispensing his medicine with a gentle pawky humour and a healing faith. A fellow prisoner, John Perrett, became interested in biology through his experiences in camp where he learned to make medicines from the resources at hand. After the war he went to Cambridge and graduated with honours in science. Recently he demonstrated before the Royal Society a process whereby bacteria can be grown speedily and diluted at the same time as they are multiplying.

George Winston before the war was a sergeant in the regular Artillery. Now, as vice-president of the Chemico Laboratories in Florida, he is working in the field of virus diseases. Recently he introduced a new drug, Reticulose, which he hopes will prove effective against virus-caused infections.

Sir Albert Coates, who did such brilliant work as a medical officer at Nakawm Paton, is today Professor of Surgery at Melbourne University. M. F. A. Woodruff, another MO, is Professor of Surgery at Edinburgh University. Ronald Searle, a famous cartoonist for *Punch, Holiday, Life* and other magazines on both sides of the Atlantic, began his career by sketching both the horrors and the lighter side of life in the South-East Asia prison camps.

Many stories of achievements at humbler levels have come to my attention. At my daily company parade there was an Argyll who used to appear every Thursday morning as regular as clockwork, charged with some offence or other by the Red Caps. His conduct sheet was as long as one's arm. I didn't meet him again until some time later when I was at Paisley. He was looking prosperous and contented. When we shook hands, the first words he said to me were, 'You'll not believe it – I'm never in trouble now.'

He went on, with great pride, to tell me of his happy marriage, how he had started a small business which was succeeding very well and how he was extremely active in community affairs.

'Do you go to church?' I asked.

'Och, aye,' he answered, to my astonishment. 'And, what's more, my name is up for the next lot of elders.'

Another POW, a fine, handsome man, was engaged to be married. He was the last surviving male of his family, his two brothers having been killed in action and his father in an air raid. He returned home to find his mother a chronic invalid and his sister tubercular from her service in the Auxiliary Territorial Service. The last I heard of him he had given up all thoughts of marriage and was taking his mother and sister out to New Zealand where he would be better able to care for them.

Welfare and other charitable organizations have benefited from the zeal and enthusiasm of men like Stewart E. Bell, an Edinburgh advocate and an elder in St Cuthbert's Church. And there are many others whose zest for good works continues to show in their numerous extra-curricular welfare activities.

Associations of former POWs sprang up all over Britain soon after our return. Now numbering seventy-nine, they have formed themselves into the Federation of Far Eastern Prisoners of War Clubs and Associations of Great Britain and Northern Ireland. The general aims of the FEPOWs are:

> To promote the material and spiritual welfare of all FEPOWs and the dependants of those who died in captivity or subsequently, and to represent their interests by all legal means; to preserve the sacred memory of those who died in captivity or subsequently, to perpetuate the

bonds of fellowship forged during captivity and to per-
petuate the spirit that kept us all going during the years
of imprisonment.

One of the objectives accomplished was to urge the Government to seek compensation from the Japanese for the brut-
alities inflicted on us. This amounted to fifteen pounds, or
forty-two dollars, for each of us. The sum was purely nominal;
nevertheless, the principle had been established that never
again should helpless POWs be treated as the Japanese military
had treated us. When this motion was debated in the House it
was opposed by many MPs on the ground that troops were
expected to undergo such suffering. It was part of a soldier's
pay.

Much more than financial help has been extended by former
POWs to one another. They have been unstinting in the giving
of their time, energy, service and counsel in every field of
endeavour, from housing to educational, religious or family
problems.

On the whole, they seem to have made much more of a
success of their lives in the difficult post-war period than those
who had an easier time of it. This is borne out by a recent
survey conducted by Dr E. P. Routley, also a former POW. Dr
Routley found that more of them have married than in other
comparable groups and that their marriages have been more
lasting. But statistics cannot tell us much of fears overcome, of
aspirations realized, of the seeds of faith, hope and love which
lodged in their hearts to flower later in the lives of others.

I, too, sought an opportunity to put my experience to work.
I had seen at first hand the cruelty of a totalitarian regime. I
knew something of suffering and what it meant to look death
in the face. I knew the depths to which men could sink and the
heights to which they could rise. I could speak knowledgeably
of despair, but also of hope; of hatred, but also of love; of man

without God, but also of man sustained by God. I knew the power of the demonic, and I knew the greater power of the Holy Spirit.

So many of the prisoners who had died in camp had been so young. I had felt their deaths keenly. I wanted ultimately to minister to the young, to those of college age. But I saw no way that my wish was to be achieved. While I was still in the United States, after I had completed my graduate studies at Hartford Theological Seminary, I told the executive secretary to the Board of Education of the Presbyterian Church about my desire to work with students. He suggested that I keep in touch with him. I returned to Scotland to do further work in history and to serve as assistant minister in the historic Abbey of Paisley. Three years went by, then at the urging of the Education Board secretary I resigned my post at the abbey and returned to the United States.

I landed in New York without any charge or parish or definite prospect of any kind. I had my sympathetic wife, my children and two hundred dollars to my name. Within a week I was invited to supply the Presbyterian churches of Amagansett and Montauk, neighbouring villages at the eastern end of Long Island. Less than a year later I was in sight of the opportunity I had been seeking. I was called to be Presbyterian pastor at Princeton University. The following year I became Dean of the Chapel.

Here I found that although prison camp and campus were poles apart, many of the questions asked me were identical to those I had been called upon to answer in South-East Asia. The miracle I knew in the jungle was being repeated daily on the campus – the miracle of God at work in His world. I recalled that when I was at Paisley I had been told how the old-time weavers, all the while they were making their beautiful and intricate patterns, saw no more than a tangle of coloured threads. They never saw the design until they took the finished fabric from their looms. The parallel to the mortal lot is plain. Human experience appears to us – as the shawls did to the weavers – to be no more than incomprehensible tangles of coloured threads, whereas in fact life represents the ordered threads in a great design – the design being woven on the loom of eternity. Looking back, in all the chaos and confusion, I could see a splendid purpose being worked out.

In my time of decision, nature and reason were neutral. They did not speak to me of anything that made possible a significant understanding of myself and my fellow man. They did not show me the vision of the Infinitely Great. Jesus, however, had spoken to me, had convinced me of the love of God and had drawn me into a meaningful fellowship with other men as brothers. Because of Him I had come to see the world in a new way as the creation of God – not purposeless but purposeful. He had opened me to life and life to me.

In the prison camp we had discovered nothing new. The grace we had experienced is the same in every generation and must be received afresh in every age. The odyssey of the spirit is eternal: there are many resting-places but no terminals. That is why the Letter to the Hebrews says, 'For here we have no continuing city, but seek one to come.'

As we journey we are all involved in the 'Great Debate' which has for its theme the age-old problems of mankind: human destiny, suffering, good and evil, freedom, sin, salvation, faith and God. Perhaps we were able to enter the debate more wholeheartedly than most, for we went in stripped for action. We were put on our own before our enemy, our neighbour, and our God, without protection from society.

But the degree of intensity with which the Debate continues – for it always has and always will – depends upon the quality of the response we are prepared to make. Being forced to face life in the raw may help one to understand the nature of the Debate, but that isn't necessary. Every person who uses the talents God gave him so that he is not afraid to live as a sensitive human being among the impersonal forces at work in society is participating and will be conscious of its only possible conclusion.

As I journey with those of the Way I see that the victory over the impersonal, destructive and enslaving forces at work in the world has been given to mankind because of what Jesus has done. This is the good news for man: God, in Christ, has shared his suffering; for that is what God is like. He has not shunned the responsibility of freedom. He shares in the saddest and most painful experiences of His children, even that experience which seems to defeat us all, namely, death.

He comes into our Death House to lead us through it.

ACKNOWLEDGEMENTS

I never seriously considered writing a book about my experience as a prisoner of war of the Japanese until it was suggested that I did so by Clarence W. Hall, senior editor of _The Reader's Digest_. This was the result of an interview he had with me which was published in the June 1960, issue of the magazine as an article entitled 'It Happened on the River Kwai'. The response to the article was sufficient to indicate there might be a place for such a book. My reason for writing it is principally that it deals with the great issues of human experience which are never old, never dated. To live life in the personal dimension is to be involved with such issues. They are inescapable. All of us are on an Odyssey, for we are all wanderers, seeking a way. Those of us who were prisoners of the Japanese were very conscious of this truth.

I am grateful to those who have urged me to write this book: to my good friend Stewart E. Bell of Edinburgh for keeping me up to date on the careers of other former POWs; to Mrs Mathilde E. Finch for her kindness in reading the first draft, and to Edward R. Sammis for his patience and enthusiasm in his work as consulting editor.

E.G.